Predictable Ops

Leading IT in the Age of AI

Robert Seeman

Predictable Ops: Leading IT in the Age of AI

Robert Seeman
San Jose, CA, USA

ISBN-13 (pbk): 979-8-8688-2024-3   ISBN-13 (electronic): 979-8-8688-2025-0
https://doi.org/10.1007/979-8-8688-2025-0

Copyright © 2025 by Robert Seeman

This work is subject to copyright. All rights are reserved by the Publisher, whether the whole or part of the material is concerned, specifically the rights of translation, reprinting, reuse of illustrations, recitation, broadcasting, reproduction on microfilms or in any other physical way, and transmission or information storage and retrieval, electronic adaptation, computer software, or by similar or dissimilar methodology now known or hereafter developed.

Trademarked names, logos, and images may appear in this book. Rather than use a trademark symbol with every occurrence of a trademarked name, logo, or image we use the names, logos, and images only in an editorial fashion and to the benefit of the trademark owner, with no intention of infringement of the trademark.

The use in this publication of trade names, trademarks, service marks, and similar terms, even if they are not identified as such, is not to be taken as an expression of opinion as to whether or not they are subject to proprietary rights.

While the advice and information in this book are believed to be true and accurate at the date of publication, neither the authors nor the editors nor the publisher can accept any legal responsibility for any errors or omissions that may be made. The publisher makes no warranty, express or implied, with respect to the material contained herein.

>   Managing Director, Apress Media LLC: Welmoed Spahr
>   Acquisitions Editor: Shivangi Ramachandran
>   Development Editor: James Markham
>   Project Manager: Jessica Vakili

Distributed to the book trade worldwide by Springer Science+Business Media New York, 1 New York Plaza, New York, NY 10004. Phone 1-800-SPRINGER, fax (201) 348-4505, e-mail orders-ny@springer-sbm.com, or visit www.springeronline.com. Apress Media, LLC is a Delaware LLC and the sole member (owner) is Springer Science + Business Media Finance Inc (SSBM Finance Inc). SSBM Finance Inc is a **Delaware** corporation.

For information on translations, please e-mail booktranslations@springernature.com; for reprint, paperback, or audio rights, please e-mail bookpermissions@springernature.com.

Apress titles may be purchased in bulk for academic, corporate, or promotional use. eBook versions and licenses are also available for most titles. For more information, reference our Print and eBook Bulk Sales web page at http://www.apress.com/bulk-sales.

If disposing of this product, please recycle the paper

To my wife. She's been through the entire journey with me and has always been a loving and understanding partner. Year after year, she's dealt with my intensity and supported my insane work schedule. I could not have done any of this without her. I am grateful beyond words.

This dedication is playing just for you.

Table of Contents

About the Author xi

About the Technical Reviewer xiii

Acknowledgments xv

Introduction xvii

Chapter 1: Rule #1—Operations Should Be Boring 1

Reliability in the Age of Autonomy 1

Where to Start 3

    Support Availability 4

    Service Downtime 7

    Service Resiliency 9

    Service Performance 10

    Efficiency—Unfriendly Tools 12

    The Worst of All Worlds 13

    Real World Example—Make the Phone Stop Ringing 15

    Predictable AI Tools That Already Work 16

Create a Culture of Documentation 17

    Real World Example—Documenting for Compliance 19

Predictability Through Tooling 20

    Key Tooling Categories for Predictable Ops 20

Chapter Summary—Rule #1—Operations Should Be Boring 22

TABLE OF CONTENTS

Chapter 2: Rule #2 Measure What Matters 25
KPIs, Metrics, and Machine Learning 25
The KPI Trap 28
KPIs vs. Metrics—The Important Distinction 29
Identifying Your KPIs 30
    Know Your Space.. 31
    Understand Your Customers 32
    Start Small 34
    Standardize Your Tracking Tools 35
    Review on a Standard Cadence 37
Dashboards and the Illusion of Control 40
    What True Observability Looks Like 41
    Predictable Ops Perspective 41
AI-Enabled Insights: From Data Display to Decision Support 43
    Dashboards Without AI 43
    Dashboards with AI 43
    How AI Ingests Observability Tools 44
Enhancing Insight with Retrieval-Augmented Generation (RAG) 46
    Example Applications 47
AI Governance—Avoid Blind Faith 47
Problem Management (aka Fixing What Broke) 49
    Predictable Ops Means Persistent Fixes 49
    AI Accelerates Root Cause—If You Let It 50
    Problem Management As a Trust Multiplier 50
Chapter Summary—Rule #2—Measure What Matters 52

TABLE OF CONTENTS

Chapter 3: Rule #3—Develop Your Team 53
Training Humans for a World of Machines 53
The Reality Shift 54
Understanding What Your "Team" Really Is 55
  Partners vs. Vendors 55
  Work Partners 55
Start with Accountability 57
AI Transition Note—The Evolution of Accountability with AI 59
  Past Operations 59
  AI-Enabled Operations 60
  Be Available 61
Trust and Support Your Team 63
  Take the Bullets 64
  Give Advice 64
  Mentor Their Mistakes 65
  Reward Ideas and Improvements 67
Track Capabilities 68
  Real World Example—Evaluating the Front Line 70
Hire for the Gaps 71
  Upskilling for AI 73
Fear of Change vs. Empowerment 75
Chapter Summary—Rule #3—Develop Your Team 77

Chapter 4: Rule #4—Know What It Costs 79
The Economics of IT Services 79
The Predictable Path Forward 81
Budget Accountability Is Team Accountability 84
Costs Always Increase 84

TABLE OF CONTENTS

Real World Example: A Cloud Reality Check 87
Real World Example—Licensing Increase 88
Beware False Savings—The Assumption Failure 89
    Use AI to Test These Assumptions Faster 90
Vendor Relationships 91
Understand Your Contracts 94
Return on Investment (ROI) 96
    Key ROI Factors for IT Investment 96
Forecasting Costs with AIOps, Analytics, and Generative AI 98
Chapter Summary—Rule #4—Know What It Costs 100

Chapter 5: Rule #5—Communication Is Essential 103
Transparency in the Black Box Era 103
Know Your Audience 105
Set the Cadence: Deadlines and Business Reviews 107
    Committing to Deadlines 108
    Meet the Date 108
    Inform Before You Miss 109
    Reviews with the Business 111
Planned Disruptions—Maintenance Schedules 113
    Real World Example: Patching the Unpatchable 114
Unplanned Outages: Speak First, Fix Fast 117
Technology Changes 118
IT Policies and Governance 120
    Common IT Policy and Compliance Frameworks 121
AI Transformation: A New Kind of Change 122
    Old Tech Change vs. AI Transformation 123
Chapter Summary—Rule #5—Communication Is Essential 124

TABLE OF CONTENTS

Chapter 6: Rule #6—Be a Trusted Partner 127

Collaborating with AI and Everyone Else 127
Predictability Builds Confidence, Confidence Enables Evolution 129
Beyond Performance—The Human Connection 131
    Real World Example—Repairing a Relationship 132
Building Personal Trust—Show Up, Speak Honestly, Ask for Help 133
Build Relationships 134
Trust Is a Prerequisite to Transformation 137
Aligning on Priorities 138
Delivering Major Initiatives: The Ultimate Trust Builder 141
    Real World Example: Partnering for Major Transformation 142
The AI Pitch 143
    Leading the AI Journey 146
Chapter Summary—Rule #6: Be a Trusted Partner 148

Chapter 7: Rule #7—Prepare for the Future 151

The Future Is Already Here! Now What? 151
Remain Up-to-Date and Modern 153
Plug into the Future of *Your* Business 156
AI: Your Bridge Between Trends and Business Value 157
Don't Fall for Trend Traps 160
Build a Roadmap 162
    Roadmap Foundations by Rule 163
    Define a Finish Line 164
    Include Your Extended Team 165
    From Experiment to Operational Reality 166
    Real World Example—From On-Prem to Cloud-First 167

TABLE OF CONTENTS

AI Transformation 168
    Stepping into the Future of IT Operations 168
Chapter Summary—Rule #7—Prepare for the Future 169

Chapter 8: Rule #8—Be Decisive 171
Connect the Predictable Ops Rules 172
Setting the Direction 175
Course Correcting 176
Standing Your Ground 178
    Real World Example—The Rules and the Tracks in Action 179
    Real World Example—The Cost of Indecision 180
The Decisive Loop 181
    1. Sense 181
    2. Decide 181
    3. Act 181
    4. Adapt 182
    Team-Level Decisiveness 183
Being Decisive in the Age of AI 183
Chapter Summary: Rule #8—Be Decisive 185

Conclusion—Leading Predictability in an Unpredictable World 187

Predictable Ops Field Guide 195

Appendix A: AI, ML, and Deep Learning Tools for the Predictable Ops Journey 211

Appendix B: AI in Action 219

Appendix C: Forms, Templates, and Tables 231

Index 241

About the Author

Robert Seeman has 30+ years of experience in IT operations leadership, overseeing major transformations from on-prem infrastructure to cloud-based platforms, multi-million-dollar cost modeling, and AI-driven Ops tools. He is a trusted advisor on vendor negotiations, service resiliency, and real-world team accountability. He is an author and speaker on practical frameworks for operations leaders who need to build trust, stability, and foresight in the Age of AI.

About the Technical Reviewer

Massimo Nardone has more than 30 years of experience in information and cybersecurity for IT/OT/IoT/IIoT, web/mobile development, cloud, and IT architecture. His true IT passions are security and Android. He holds an M.Sc. in Computing Science from the University of Salerno, Italy.

Throughout his working career, he has held various positions starting as programming developer, then security teacher, PCI QSA, auditor, assessor, lead IT/OT/SCADA/cloud architect, CISO, BISO, executive, program director, OT/IoT/IIoT security competence leader, etc. In his last working engagement, he worked as a seasoned cyber and information security executive, CISO, and OT, IoT, and IIoT security competence leader, helping many clients to develop and implement cyber, information, OT, and IoT security activities.

He is currently working as Vice President of OT Security for SSH Communications Security.

Acknowledgments

I could write an entire book about those who have been an important factor in my career. A leader is the product of their team and their partners, and I have been blessed to both work with and lead many talented and brilliant professionals. I've also been fortunate to grow under phenomenal mentors and leaders, who cared enough to invest their time, effort, and experience in me.

I wish I could name each of you and recognize the tremendous contributions you've made. Please know that I remember it all, and I appreciate every one of you.

Introduction

Why Are We Here?

Operational intelligence has shaped industry, warfare, espionage, and countless coordinated human endeavors for as long as recordkeeping has existed. Throughout history, the practice of gathering and applying operational insight has undergone numerous inflection points. Today, in the mid-2020s, we are living through one of the most profound of those transformations: the rise of Artificial Intelligence.

Companies across every sector are investing heavily in AI, drawn by its promises of efficiency, speed, and competitive advantage. Yet with this excitement comes uncertainty. How do we, as IT professionals, navigate a world where strategic decisions are increasingly shaped or even made by AI systems?

In my estimation, the answer is deceptively simple: **apply what we know works, through the lens of modern tools.** This approach has been a constant throughout decades of evolution in Information Technology. Whether we were adopting virtualization, embracing the cloud, or now experimenting with generative AI, the underlying principles of sound operations have remained timeless.

This book is a collection of hard-won insights about running IT operations. Lessons discovered over decades of practice. For experienced executives, you may find confirmation of what you've long known to be true. For newer professionals, perhaps a spark that shapes your leadership journey.

INTRODUCTION

These insights are not frozen in time. They are intended to evolve alongside the industry itself. Throughout the chapters ahead, you'll see how core operational principles remain relevant in this rapidly changing AI and IT landscape. In fact, these principles remain vital.

I've been fortunate to experience and learn a lot over the course of my career with much of it through trial and error. Early on, I had mentors who were patient enough to see me through those trials, helping me grow. My hope is that by sharing my story, I can spare you some of the pain I went through. If even one person finds value in these lessons, then writing this book will have been worth the effort.

I truly want you to learn from me, as best you can. Some of my failures were painful. At times, even soul-sucking. But they were also incredibly formative. If my experiences can save you even a little bit of that hardship, I'll be grateful. The truths I've learned were relevant in the 1990s, during Y2K, through the Dot-Com crash, the Financial Crisis, the COVID-19 pandemic, and I believe they will remain relevant no matter how technology evolves.

This world has been my home for more than three decades. I'm excited to open the door and welcome you in. Look around. Take what makes sense. Leave with whatever you find useful.

Why Predictability Still Matters—Even Now
Be Predictable

The technology landscape is always shifting beneath our feet. It's an amorphous swirl of breakthroughs, evolving industry demands, and relentless competitive pressure. In short, it has always been, and likely always will be, the antithesis of predictability.

So why would a book about *predictable* IT operations matter now?

Because in the chaos of constant change, in the fog of uncertainty, **leaders who are reliable, relatable, and yes… PREDICTABLE** are the ones people seek out to make sense of it all. In an era of rapidly advancing automation and AI-driven decision-making, **predictable operations are no longer optional—they're essential**.

You can't outsource discipline. You can't automate leadership. You have to build it.

You've come to the right place to learn how.

In this book, we'll explore how transforming and sustaining Predictable IT Operations can elevate you to one of the most trusted and respected leaders in any organization, and prepare you now for the **Age of AI**.

IT operations have undergone radical shifts in recent decades. The pace of change is only accelerating. Leaders and their teams have had to continuously evolve both mindset and skill set. The move to cloud platforms demanded a transformation from physical infrastructure to virtual, from hardware to infrastructure-as-code. DevOps initiatives required full-stack thinking and blurred the lines of traditional roles. Now, **AI has arrived**, bringing with it new expectations around automation, data fluency, and adaptive decision-making.

Just as with previous paradigm shifts (Cloud, DevOps, and others), a solid, predictable operational foundation is the *essential* ingredient for navigating AI transformation. AI is not a magic wand; it's an accelerant. It amplifies whatever it touches.

In IT operations, that means AI will **enhance strength where strength already exists**—but it will just as quickly **expose weaknesses with brutal clarity**. The teams that have built structure, discipline, and reliability into their practices will scale faster and smarter. The ones operating in chaos will only accelerate their own dysfunction.

A Word of Caution before we see AI as a pool into which we can simply dive head-first. **AI is not just a technical tool, it's a business risk surface.** Many organizations are understandably cautious about deploying AI

INTRODUCTION

agents, generative models, and automated remediation tools. Concerns around copyright, data leakage, IP protection, and trade secrets are real. That's why Predictable Leaders **work with AI Councils, Legal, and Security** teams to ensure responsible AI usage. Operational excellence means building trust, and trust begins with clear policies, controlled rollouts, partnership and transparency in how AI is applied.

The Predictable Leader understands the challenges mentioned above and embraces them. Yet many professionals equate being "predictable" with being stagnant or inflexible. Nothing could be further from the truth. As you'll see, a truly predictable leader isn't afraid of change—they *master* it. They're the ones best equipped to drive improvement, recognize opportunity, and lead through disruption.

Narrative Structure

This book is organized around narrative themes, each structured as a **Rule**. Throughout each chapter, we'll explore why that Rule matters and how it shapes the Predictable leader's toolkit. You'll also see how these principles tie directly into the AI journey ahead.

Appendix B offers a concise summary of how each Rule connects to practical AI tools, use cases, and prompts you can apply in your own organization.

The Rules follow two interconnected tracks that reflect the core transformation of Predictable IT leadership:

Track 1 – Operational Trust

These chapters build the culture and practices that earn confidence from your business, customers, and peers:

- **Rule #1 – Operations Should Be Boring**
- **Rule #3 – Develop Your Team**

- Rule #5 – Communication Is Essential
- Rule #6 – Be a Trusted Partner

Track 2 – Preparation and Foresight

These chapters focus on equipping yourself and your team with the right structure, measurements, and mindset to lead effectively:

- Rule #2 – Measure What Matters
- Rule #4 – Know What It Costs
- Rule #7 – Prepare for the Future

Final Convergence

The two tracks come together in the final chapter:

- Rule #8 – Be Decisive
  - Where preparation and trust form the basis of strong, timely leadership, especially in the age of AI.

These Rules aren't just theory but a working model. Together, they form the blueprint of Predictable Ops and prepare you to lead your organization through its next transformation.

Rule #1: Operations Should Be Boring (Reliability in the Age of Autonomy)

You are a service provider. When your services and the experiences they enable vary from day to day, you become instantly untrustworthy. Reliability to the point of being *boring* is the foundation of Predictable IT Operations.

INTRODUCTION

Rule #2: Measure What Matters (KPIs, Metrics, and Machine Learning)
Predictability is only reachable when you measure it. The performance data you collect not only shows if you are meeting your goals, it provides information for critical decisions. It is therefore critical to track Key Performance Indicators that give you the information you need to track your journey to Predictability, to highlight what is working, and to expose what is standing in your way.

Rule #3: Develop Your Team (Training Humans for a World of Machines)
Too many leaders treat team development as a checkbox: send someone to training, get a certification, and consider the job done. But true development is more complex. It requires building trust, setting clear expectations, holding people accountable, creating space for growth, and aligning personal development with business objectives.

As IT operations evolve, so must your team. The coming years will demand more than technical know-how. Your people will need deep data literacy, the ability to work alongside AI, and the skills to translate machine insights into human decisions. This is not optional. If you want Predictable Ops in the age of AI, you must start with a team built for it.

Rule #4: Know What It Costs (The Economics of IT Services)
Surprisingly, many leaders don't have the slightest clue how much it actually costs to deliver their services. This creates the illusion, or worse, the delusion, that those services are somehow "free." In traditional IT, in the Cloud, and now with AI platforms, cost ignorance isn't just a gap but a leadership failure.

AI has the potential to model your costs more accurately (and, yes, predictively), but only if you've already done the work of capturing those costs in the first place.

Rule #5: Communication Is Essential (Transparency in a Black Box Era)

Your communication style needs to be as Predictable as your services. When IT touches things, they often break. No world exists in which computer systems are perfect. In the Age of AI, this gets even more complex as decisions become more opaque.

Rule #6: Be a Trusted Partner (Collaborating with AI—And Everyone Else)

A Predictable Leader seeks out challenges and actively partners with colleagues to solve them. As AI becomes an essential part of how we plan, operate, and deliver, the most Predictable force in your organization must still be you. Trust is more than just being there when things break. Trust is built by proving you can construct what comes next. Delivering day-to-day builds credibility. Delivering the big bets cements trust that you can help the business grow. You need to do more than just keep the lights on.

Rule #7: Prepare for the Future (The Future Is Already Here—Now What?)

IT is never "future proof." Your business partners, vendors, industry, even technology itself will leave you behind if you're not actively tracking the trends that shape our world. Everything from cloud platforms to infrastructure as code to the holy grail of artificial intelligence is evolving faster than most realize. Preparing for the future is about making the brave, practical moves that position your Ops for what's next while still delivering today.

Rule #8: Be Decisive (Leadership Despite Ambiguity)

Many leaders float on a breeze, offering little direction to their team. The Predictable Leader does not shift their stance based on what's forced upon them, nor do they consistently fail to provide clarity or act without conviction. Decisive leaders don't just accept their mistakes, they **own them**, correct them, and restore Predictability as fast as possible.

INTRODUCTION

Conclusion: Leading Predictability in an Unpredictable World
At the end of this journey, we reflect on a few key aspects. There are certain operational truths that are timeless and fundamental to success in IT Leadership. AI doesn't replace operational excellence; it will amplify its consequences. Confident, human-centered leadership augmented by powerful tools is the gateway to leadership in the era of AI.

Sidebar: Take a Risk
Each Rule is governed by an immutable truth. That is, we must be prepared to take calculated risks. Throughout the chapters as we discuss the Rules, we will highlight important risks that we must be willing to address, calculate, and oftentimes embrace.

Sidebar: Prompt the AI
In each section, we will examine opportunities to take the lessons learned, the data gathered, and other sources of information, to develop AI Prompts. These sidebars will show you how to apply AI to the discussed skills.

Appendix
At the end of this book, you will find a number of forms/cheat sheets that align with the Rules discussions. Each form is numbered based on the Rule they reference. For example, Form 1.1 relates to Rule #1. Form 3.2 relates to Rule #3, and is the second piece of collateral that references that Rule. You might find that several of these forms are already available to you through tools or reports in your business environment. Use these forms as you deem them relevant to your operations.

Predictable Ops Field Guide
This Field Guide is designed to help you put the Rules into practice, one decision at a time. Use these short worksheets, reflection prompts, and "Try It This Week" actions to guide your teams, run your operations more predictably, and build trust and foresight in everything you do. Each Field Guide entry links back to one of the two major Tracks: Operational Trust or

Preparation and Foresight. The Guide ties together the ideas and sidebars you've seen throughout the book. Keep it at your desk, share it with your team, and revisit it every time the landscape shifts. Predictable Ops is something you practice, not just design.

The Bridge to AI
Predictable Ops is the foundation for a successful transformation into the Age of AI. The road ahead is built on three essential components: trust in your operations, preparation for the future, and the fortitude to be **that** leader when it matters most.

This framework and the discipline it demands equips you with the mindset, the skillset, the datasets, the toolset, and the relationships you'll need to lead confidently into the future. The future is AI and the future is NOW. We will build the bridge to AI together throughout this book.

As we explore each of these Rules, you'll see how becoming a Predictable Leader builds that bridge for you, your team, and your business, not just into the Age of AI, but into whatever comes next.

CHAPTER 1

Rule #1—Operations Should Be Boring

Reliability in the Age of Autonomy

You are a service provider. When your services and the experiences they enable vary from day to day, you become instantly untrustworthy. Reliability to the point of being boring is the foundation of Predictable IT Operations.

The holy grail of Predictable IT Operations is when services work transparently for your customers and are consistently manageable for your team. In other words, when operations become so reliable, they're boring. If your operations are quiet, your teams aren't firefighting, and your customers aren't complaining, then you're doing something incredibly right.

Indeed, you are not in the business of fixing things. You are in the business of ensuring your services work, and stay working.

Many IT leaders and engineers take pride in their ability to fix things when they break. The adrenaline, the hero moments, the "I saved the day" feeling can be very addictive. In reality, that same instinct often fuels instability. While you might believe you're a rock star for jumping on issues as they arise, you're actually sustaining the chaos that makes organizations dysfunctional. The real hero is the one whose systems don't break in the first place.

CHAPTER 1   RULE #1—OPERATIONS SHOULD BE BORING

AI will not fix this mindset. In fact, when misapplied, it can *amplify* it, automating responses to symptoms without ever addressing root causes. Feeding AI into a reactive culture only speeds up the dysfunction.

To be clear, **implementing AI Ops doesn't imply immediate disruption and chaos**. Stability still wins. The real opportunity is to use AI as a tool for proactive resilience: to predict failures before they occur, surface hidden patterns in behavior, and enable intelligent alerting.

The leader who breaks the reactive cycle and builds a system that runs *predictably*, with or without human intervention, will be seen as a game changer.

This Rule is your foundation for *Operational Trust* **(Track 1)**. Calm, stable operations earn the credibility and trust to innovate, because it demonstrates to your teams and partners they can count on you when it matters.

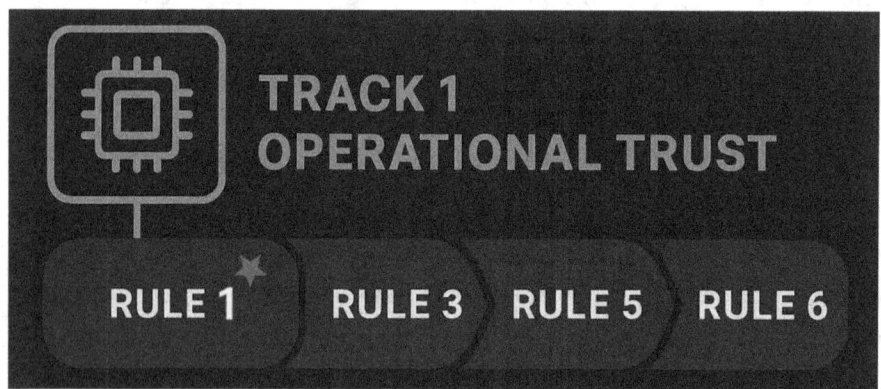

CHAPTER 1   RULE #1—OPERATIONS SHOULD BE BORING

Chapter Topics—Rule #1— Operations Should Be Boring

- Where to Start
- Predictability 101
    - Support Availability
    - Service Downtime and Resiliency
    - Service Performance
    - Efficiency of Tools
- Building a Culture of Documentation
- Predictability Through Tooling
- Take a Risk and Prompt the AI
- Chapter Summary

Where to Start

Whether you're a new leader inheriting a team, an established leader looking to level up, or someone preparing to implement AI-assisted remediation, your first step should be the same: **identify what's not working**.

Ask yourself two foundational questions:

- What is my **team** complaining about?
- What are my **customers** complaining about?

If you're hearing constant noise from either group, that's your signal. You're not failing at innovation, you're failing at **Predictability 101**.

These complaints usually fall into a small number of repeatable patterns:

- **Support Availability** – Systems may be up, but help isn't accessible when it's needed most.

- **Service Downtime** – Outages or failures erode trust quickly, especially if they're recurring.

- **Service Performance** – Sluggish systems don't just hurt productivity, they hurt credibility.

- **Efficiency/Hard to Use** – If services are clunky or unintuitive, people will find workarounds—or worse, avoid them entirely.

These are the friction points AI won't fix for you. In fact, they're exactly the kind of pain points AI will **amplify** if you try to automate over dysfunction. That's why your baseline must be solid. AI rewards strength and punishes chaos.

Let's review these in detail.

Support Availability

The first category of complaint every IT leader must address is bidirectional: the *availability of support*. This is a pain point not just for your customers as it often frustrates your frontline engineers even more.

"I'm the only one who knows how to fix this!" – Team

"It takes forever to get someone to help!" – Customer

"I'm stuck on this issue and no one's stepping in!" – Team

We'll dive deeper into building team capability in **Rule #3**, but let's be clear: until you understand the pain of support gaps, both from your customers' perspective and your team's, any analysis of downtime or performance is premature.

That's why **Predictable Ops starts here**. If no one's around to pick up the phone or respond to alerts, nothing else will matter. Support *must* be available, and visibly so, before IT can become boring in the best sense of the word.

This is also where **AI Ops can have its earliest and most impactful wins**. Well-trained virtual agents, automated escalation handlers, and generative AI chatbots can significantly reduce response bottlenecks. But there's a caveat: **AI only helps when it knows what to do.**

That means the effectiveness of AI vs. human support is directly tied to the **quality of your documentation** (see *Create a Culture of Documentation*, below). Without it, AI will automate confusion instead of clarity.

Another challenge: **support availability issues are rarely tracked in ITSM systems.** Unlike obvious failures like outages or latency, support gaps often appear as frustrated emails, hallway conversations, Slack rants, or impromptu escalations in meetings, none of which are logged or tagged.

The Predictable Ops leader doesn't ignore this. You **create lightweight mechanisms** to capture these signals, be it a shared ledger, a Slack thread, or an AI-assisted feedback form. Then you analyze those complaints for patterns and **build support structures that make IT feel mundane, boring, and seamless.**

·[AI]· PROMPT THE AI—ANALYZE SUPPORT AVAILABILITY GAPS

One of the most persistent sources of operational chaos is misaligned or insufficient frontline coverage. Whether it's missed handoffs, thin weekend staffing, or overlapping schedules that waste resources, the result is the same: service disruptions and customer frustration.

AI can help uncover these gaps *before* they show up in your ticket queue.

CHAPTER 1   RULE #1—OPERATIONS SHOULD BE BORING

If you use a ticket tracking tool like **ServiceNow**, export your historical **incident and case data.** Also, if you use a shift-tracking tool such as **PagerDuty,** download your **on-call or staffing schedule.** Load this data into a readily available AI tool like ChatGPT, Copilot, or a BI/analytics engine. Then prompt:

"Acting as an IT leader responsible for support coverage…"

"Analyze this incident data and support schedule. Identify periods of heavy ticket volume with low or no coverage. Flag recurring patterns, delayed response times, or SLA breaches tied to coverage gaps."

For more proactive planning:

"Recommend schedule adjustments to improve weekday shift balance and weekend coverage. Model the impact of adding one part-time weekend agent or redistributing on-call rotations."

Or to tie into your "boring operations" goal:

"Highlight support gaps that could lead to increased escalations, repeated tickets, or system downtime. Suggest mitigation strategies to stabilize operations."

Support gaps are a leading indicator of instability. AI won't necessarily staff your team but it can give you the visibility you need to do it better.

When customers can reliably get help, and your engineers are no longer overburdened or firefighting in isolation, *that* is when Predictable Ops starts to take root.

CHAPTER 1   RULE #1—OPERATIONS SHOULD BE BORING

TAKE A RISK—BE TRANSPARENT ABOUT BURNOUT

Your team won't always tell you when they're drowning, especially if they think no one's listening.

Take the risk of **inviting candid feedback** about workload and fatigue. Run an anonymous survey. Ask your team, "What support expectations are unrealistic?" or "Where are we failing each other?" Then share what you heard and what you plan to do.

Transparency isn't a weakness. It's leadership. **Predictable Ops is sustainable only when burnout isn't hiding beneath the surface.**

Service Downtime

When users complain about IT services, it's usually because something truly isn't working. One of the most frustrating experiences is when a service they rely on is unavailable or down. Consider these examples:

- "I can't access the finance application."
- "I can't connect to VPN."
- "Wi-Fi isn't working at my desk."
- "My print jobs aren't coming out of the printer."

There's nothing Predictable about those experiences. When they occur, the end-user's day becomes chaotic, not boring. The same goes for the support teams fielding those disruptions.

Let's be clear: Yes, there are sometimes false alarms or user misunderstandings, but they are the exception, not the rule. Dismissing a problem report as "user error" without investigation is not just disrespectful, it's dangerous. It creates blind spots in your operations and erodes trust.

CHAPTER 1 RULE #1—OPERATIONS SHOULD BE BORING

A one-off incident might not shake confidence in your services. But add a single word to the end of those same complaints, and the story changes completely:

- "I can't access the finance application…**again**."
- "I can't connect to VPN…**again**."
- "Wi-Fi isn't working at my desk…**again**."
- "My print jobs aren't coming out…**again**."

That one word—*again*—signals something far more damaging than an isolated outage. It implies a pattern. It tells your users that their frustrations are recurring, and your operations aren't improving. At that point, your services *are* Predictable but for all the wrong reasons.

Predictable IT means users don't have to think about whether things will work. They just do.

🤖 PROMPT THE AI—IDENTIFY RECURRING COMPLAINTS

Recurring complaints are rarely isolated. They're usually the symptoms of deeper systemic issues. AI can help surface those patterns faster than you can scan a spreadsheet.

If you're not using a full-featured ITSM tool yet, start with **Form 1.1—Service Complaint Ledger** (see Appendix). This basic tracker gives you a structured way to capture issue type, impacted users, date/time, location, and notes on resolution. It's simple but powerful when paired with AI.

Once you've logged enough data, upload the Ledger to a tool like ChatGPT and prompt:

"Analyze this dataset to identify recurring IT service failures. Group by service, frequency, and affected teams. Highlight issues that occur more than once per week or appear across multiple locations. Identify likely root causes based on description patterns."

You can also ask for

- **Anomaly detection** across time windows (e.g., spikes in VPN issues every Monday).
- **Trend analysis** on latency, downtime, or failed resolutions.
- **Heatmaps** of repeat problems by system, site, or shift.

AI won't solve your service issues, but it will accelerate your understanding of them. Predictable leaders use these insights to act *before* the next ticket comes in. Use the output to investigate bottlenecks before they escalate. AI helps you cut through the noise and see the patterns behind the pain.

Service Resiliency

Predictability means right-sized risk.

Predictable Ops doesn't mean every system has 100% uptime. It means your services are resilient in proportion to the risk they carry. Some systems need full clustering, failover, and geo-redundancy because they keep your business running and customers connected. Others can be less robust. That's not a flaw, that's good design.

The Predictable Leader identifies which services need what level of resilience. You don't waste money over-engineering low-risk tools but you never under-engineer critical revenue drivers or compliance-bound services. Boring means knowing where you can absorb risk, and where you can't afford surprises at all.

Form 1.2—Service Resiliency Profile—Template shows a basic outline for how to approach this question with your customers. Service downtime can frequently be directly attributable to a poor service resiliency plan.

CHAPTER 1   RULE #1—OPERATIONS SHOULD BE BORING

Keep your documentation concise. Make each survey a living doc in your CMDB, runbook, or shareable service portal. Use it to set **clear expectations** with business partners so there are no illusions about resilience levels, cost trade-offs, or recovery steps.

TAKE A RISK—BE HONEST ABOUT WHAT WILL BREAK

It's tempting to promise customers "five nines" for every service. That's a lie waiting to explode. Take the risk of telling the truth: what services will fail, how long recovery takes, and what the business impact really is. You'll spend less time over-engineering low-impact systems and have more trust when you invest heavily in the ones that matter most.

Predictable means you have the guts to tell your customers exactly what will fail, when, and why so there are no illusions when the downtime hits.

Service Performance

Short of a full outage, nothing frustrates end-users more than inconsistent or sluggish service. In fact, some users would prefer a total failure. They can stop working and escalate. But when a system is *technically up* yet *barely usable*, they're forced to struggle through degraded performance, which erodes productivity and trust.

You've heard these complaints before:

- "Why is the network always slow?"
- "This report takes forever to run every day."
- "The video freezes every time I'm on a conference call."

These aren't isolated gripes. They are early warning signs that your services are losing credibility. Performance degradation often creeps in gradually, so it can be even more corrosive than a clean outage. If not caught early, the issue becomes institutionalized. People stop reporting it. They simply work around it and lose faith in the process.

This is where **Form 1.1: Service Complaint Ledger** becomes a powerful tool. Use it to track performance complaints by system, location, or user group. Over time, you'll see patterns—and patterns reveal what's really broken. Furthermore, find opportunities to evolve this form into an enterprise tool-based system to centralize the data for long-term use.

AI-based trend analysis can enhance this further. A Predictable Leader doesn't wait for performance issues to snowball. They measure them, surface the patterns, and fix the root cause before frustration becomes the norm.

TAKE A RISK—BELIEVE THE COMPLAINTS

It's easy to dismiss complaints as noise, especially when they're inconsistent or hard to reproduce. The Predictable Leader knows that where there's smoke, there's usually fire.

Take the risk of believing your users. Assume the experience *is* bad, even if your dashboards say everything is fine. Then go deeper.

Leverage AI to analyze qualitative inputs such as user comments, ticket text, even meeting transcripts. Treat vague reports as starting points, not dead ends. You might find the issue is real, just hiding in plain sight.

Your metrics may say green. Your users say red. Trust, but verify with AI as your flashlight.

CHAPTER 1   RULE #1—OPERATIONS SHOULD BE BORING

Efficiency—Unfriendly Tools

Nothing breaks the rhythm of predictable operations faster than tools that are difficult to use. Whether it's clunky user interfaces, confusing workflows, or slow performance, inefficient tools create unnecessary friction for your customers and your team alike.

When the very systems that are supposed to support productivity become obstacles, frustration builds fast. You'll hear it in the hallways:

- "I spend more time figuring out the system than solving the problem."
- "This tool feels like it was designed by someone who's never used it."
- "Why do I need five clicks to do what used to take one?"

Too often, these complaints get brushed off. Leaders defend the tools because of sunk cost: the hours of training, the budget already spent, and the political capital used to adopt it. But defending inefficiency is defending dysfunction. If the tool no longer supports the mission or never did, it's your job to acknowledge the pain and explore solutions.

More importantly, this isn't just about listening to complaints. It's about observing behavior. Do people build spreadsheets to avoid the official dashboard? Are team members relying on side-channel chats instead of using the formal incident system? Are tasks being done manually outside of the workflow tool?

These are all signs that the tools are getting in the way. And when that happens, predictability suffers.

Your job as a leader is not to force people to love a broken tool. It's to ensure the tools support the work, not create more of it. In a Predictable Ops environment, tools should fade into the background. They should feel like part of the rhythm, not a disruption.

This is also a place where AI can help. AI-powered tools can simplify workflows, surface context-sensitive help, automate tedious steps, and even route requests based on learned behavior. But if your baseline toolset is a mess, AI will only mask the inefficiencies—not solve them.

So listen carefully. Observe behaviors. And remember: every time someone avoids the official process, they're telling you where the real friction is.

The Worst of All Worlds

It's not uncommon for all these symptoms to appear at once, especially if you've been brought in to fix things or have inherited a struggling team. This kind of situation can feel overwhelming. But it's also the clearest signal that your first job is to document everything. Thoroughly. Relentlessly. You cannot improve what you haven't clearly defined.

Think about the perception this environment creates:

- Support is limited or unreliable.
- Services are frequently unavailable.
- Performance is slow or degraded.
- Tools are difficult or confusing to use.

These are both technical problems and operational red flags. They shape the way your customers, peers, and company leaders see IT as a whole.

When you're in a situation like this, you're more than just solving outages or tuning performance. You're rebuilding trust. That trust will come from action, clarity, and measurable improvement.

In Rule #6, we'll talk about what it means to **Be a Trusted Partner.** For now, understand that tackling this chaos with a Predictable mindset by starting with honest documentation and transparency, it sets the stage for operational maturity.

CHAPTER 1   RULE #1—OPERATIONS SHOULD BE BORING

No matter how bad things seem, boring is always within reach. First, you have to name the chaos before you can calm it.

·[AI]· PROMPT THE AI—USE AI TO IDENTIFY MAJOR PAIN POINTS

Until now, identifying recurring IT issues meant exporting raw ticket data into a spreadsheet, building pivot tables, and manually scanning for patterns. That approach still works but it's slow, limited, and prone to interpretation bias.

Today, AI-assisted insight tools like ChatGPT, Copilot, or embedded AIOps modules can parse the same data in seconds and offer deeper analysis. The modern approach for many years in ticketing platforms includes built-in visualization and aggregating features that surface chronic pain points without requiring manual slicing.

When you've collected data using something like Form 1.1 or extracted a report from your ITSM system, prompt the AI with targeted questions to accelerate your insights.

Sample Prompts:

- "Given the spreadsheet I just uploaded, in which areas of IT do you see chronic issues?"
- "Do you see any correlation between seemingly unrelated reported system or process problems?"
- "Which teams seem to be having the most issues? Are the problems related to a single application or service?"

Use the AI to spot what you might have missed—and then lead the team to fix it.

CHAPTER 1   RULE #1—OPERATIONS SHOULD BE BORING

Real World Example—Make the Phone Stop Ringing

Early in my career, I worked for a stealth start-up so secretive that even most employees at the parent company didn't know we existed. That meant our small local IT team was on its own to handle every operational need.

When I joined, the start-up had been running for a couple of years. However, the IT systems were managed "by committee," mostly by engineers and QA teams focused on shipping product, not building stable Ops. On my first day, I found out from an Ops perspective that we had a "target rich environment."

Our Director of Operations, my boss's boss, gave us a clear directive: "Make the phone stop ringing." He meant it literally. He didn't want his phone to keep ringing at all hours, but it was also ***an important mindset***. Every call was a signal: a complaint, an outage, a gap in service. If the phones were ringing, we weren't predictable. If we could fix the root causes behind those calls, we'd get boring.

And that was the goal.

It wasn't easy. We had to hire more support staff to plug big support and service availability gaps. We upgraded networks and Wi-Fi that were stable but severely underperforming. We modernized primitive tooling. And every fix got us closer.

We measured our progress with new KPIs and strict SLAs (see Rule #2), but the mantra never changed: "Make the phone stop ringing." Over time, that simple operational truth taught me what Predictable Ops really is: when things work so well, nobody feels the need to complain, or even notice. **Boring is beautiful.**

 ## Predictable AI Tools That Already Work

AI in operations isn't a futuristic dream. It's already making today's environments more predictable. From anomaly detection and automated escalations to full-blown autonomous actions, AI tooling is quietly reshaping how issues are prevented and resolved.

The irony? The most advanced tools are often the ones making things less exciting, and that's a win.

Think about it: systems that detect a pattern and act on it before a human ever logs in. Dashboards that surface the root cause rather than a wall of alerts. Assistants that summarize trends from thousands of tickets in seconds.

These tools don't just reduce noise; they reduce risk. They free your team from reactive chaos and let them focus on high-value work. When operations become that stable, that *boring*, then you're doing something right.

Appendix A—AI, ML, and Deep Learning Tools has a full list of tools that you can pilot or perhaps might already be leveraging. Some examples of areas that can be automated or enhanced with AI tools include

- *Splunk ITSI* – Detect anomalies across metrics and logs.
- *BigPanda* – Correlate incidents and reduce alert fatigue.
- *Microsoft CoPilot + ServiceNow* – AI summaries, suggestions, and automated responses.
- *ChatOps with SlackGPT/Teams* – Natural language queries like "show open incidents with database errors in the last 48 hours."

Create a Culture of Documentation

To achieve boring, predictable operations, you must create a culture of documentation. This isn't just about having a few process guides lying around. It's about setting the standard: "If it isn't written down, it doesn't exist."

AI-assisted remediation, in particular, *requires* boring, predictable inputs to avoid overcorrection. AI thrives on clear structure. It can only help you based on the information you give it, so if your documentation is missing, outdated, or chaotic, the AI's output will be, too.

Even without AI in the picture, solid documentation is a hallmark of a mature operations team. **But with AI in the loop, it becomes non-negotiable.**

The Predictable Leader invests in documentation not as a one-time effort, but as a living, breathing part of the team's workflow. Key documentation categories include

- **Runbooks** – Step-by-step instructions for common operational tasks, including preventive maintenance and incident response.

- **Policies** – Standards and expectations for how IT resources are used and governed.

- **Diagrams** – Architecture maps, business workflows, application dependencies, data center layouts, and just about anything that provides visual clarity into how systems connect and operate.

- **Ticketing Systems** – Trouble tickets, change records, and vendor interactions that form a critical record of what's happening across the environment.

CHAPTER 1   RULE #1—OPERATIONS SHOULD BE BORING

A hard-and-fast rule that all Predictable leaders should incorporate into their policies is this: **If it's not documented, it doesn't exist.** Indeed, AI makes the need for this work even more valuable. Well-documented systems allow AI to automate with confidence, highlight anomalies, and reduce your team's manual burden. However, without documentation, the AI is flying blind. Which means, so are you.

·[AI]· PROMPT THE AI—AUTOMATE WITH DOCUMENTATION

AI can only act on what you've told it. AI guessing or "hallucinations" are dangerous. That's why clean, consistent documentation is the foundation for AI-assisted remediation. Once that foundation is built, you can prompt AI tools to perform useful tasks like

- "Use the runbook library to generate a remediation sequence for common VPN failures."
- "Analyze incident tickets from the last 90 days and recommend updates to the escalation SOP."
- "Suggest missing runbooks based on repeated service issues in the last quarter."
- "Review architecture diagrams and flag inconsistencies between our CMDB and production topology."

AI needs clarity to be useful. If your documentation is solid, AI can scale your efforts. If your documentation is messy, AI will just scale your chaos.

Build the docs first. Then ask the AI.

Real World Example—Documenting for Compliance

In some cases, documentation isn't just good practice. It's a legal or industry requirement. Now, more than ever before, audit-and-compliance is an overarching imperative in IT. In my career, I've regularly had to engage in annual audits related to SOX, NIST, ISO-9xxx, TISAX—name your acronym and I've likely dealt with it. In each case, documentation of "process and proof" has been essential.

One such audit required evidence of administrative access controls to financial systems. The auditors weren't just checking who had access; they wanted detailed documentation of who approved it, when it was last reviewed, and what process was used to validate continued need. In environments like this, undocumented actions might as well have never happened.

Fortunately, we had built a culture that prioritized documentation as part of daily operations. Access reviews were performed quarterly and logged with workflow approvals. System changes followed formal ITIL practices, which were documented and linked to change tickets. We didn't need a fire drill to gather evidence because we already had it.

The audit concluded with no findings and a note of appreciation from the auditor on how clean and accessible our documentation package was.

A culture of documentation isn't just about protecting your operations, it's about protecting your and your company's credibility. Compliance doesn't reward heroics, it rewards discipline. In the **Age of AI**, that discipline must extend to how systems make decisions and how those decisions are recorded.

In the end, Predictability isn't just about keeping things running. It's about making sure your work holds up under scrutiny. When audit season comes, the team that documents is the team that sleeps.

CHAPTER 1   RULE #1—OPERATIONS SHOULD BE BORING

Predictability Through Tooling

At the heart of Predictable Ops is strong process and adherence to those processes, but the tooling that supports those processes is just as important. The best tools don't replace good process; they amplify it.

Beyond the general productivity applications your customers use (as discussed earlier), the tools you use to manage, monitor, and evolve your services have a direct and vital role in delivering "boring" services. The right tools create consistency. The wrong tools (or too many tools) create confusion.

Key Tooling Categories for Predictable Ops

- **Ticketing Tools** – Centralize incident, request, change, and problem management. Look for features that integrate with monitoring and alerting, allow workflow automation, and provide strong reporting for trend analysis. The ability to link incidents to root cause investigations builds operational learning.

- **Automation Tools** – Enable rapid, repeatable, and error-free execution of routine tasks. Use these to scale capacity on demand, execute predefined recovery actions during service impacts, and eliminate manual steps from deployment or provisioning processes.

- **Monitoring Tools** – Your "pane of glass" for operational health. Prioritize unified monitoring over fragmented solutions. Metrics, logs, traces, and user experience data should be correlated, not siloed. Predictability depends on seeing the *whole* picture, not just isolated alerts.

- **Deployment Tools** – Reduce risk by ensuring new releases can be deployed quickly, safely, and consistently. Push-button or automated pipelines beat manual deployments every time—especially when rollbacks are just as simple.

- **Collaboration Tools** – Facilitate cross-team communication during incidents, project delivery, and service design. Integrations with ticketing, monitoring, and documentation systems keep everyone in the same context without hopping between disjointed channels.

Many IT departments, and most broader organizations for that matter, have what a former CIO of mine called a "rich application portfolio." While variety sounds appealing, a chaotic tooling environment erodes predictability. Every tool should have a clear purpose, clear owners, and a clear integration path into the broader operational workflow.

PROMPT THE AI—RATIONALIZE THE TOOL STACK

Upload your list of operational tools such as ticketing, monitoring, automation, deployment, and collaboration, along with their primary owners and use cases.

Ask AI to

> "Analyze overlap, gaps, and integration opportunities in this tooling stack. Identify tools that could be consolidated, processes that could be automated with existing tools, and any critical functions that currently have no dedicated tooling."

Tip If you're in Microsoft 365 or Google Workspace environments, explore built-in AI assistants (like Microsoft Copilot) that can surface under-used tool features before you consider buying something new.

Chapter Summary—Rule #1—Operations Should Be Boring

The most effective IT operations aren't flashy. They're stable, quiet, and uneventful. They are *boring* by design. Predictable operations begin with knowing where to start: listening to complaints, tracking patterns, and documenting what's broken. From the availability of support, to system downtime, to slow performance and confusing tools, each pain point represents a threat to stability. But these are not just technical problems; they're trust problems. Each unresolved issue erodes confidence in your team and your leadership.

To reverse this, you must commit to operational discipline. Build a culture of documentation that removes tribal knowledge and enables repeatability. Make support accessible and visible. Prioritize speed *and* consistency. And when everything is broken? Don't panic! Start tracking, start fixing, and start communicating.

AI can help but only if your foundation is solid. With clear documentation and structured inputs, AI can accelerate root cause analysis, automate resolution, and surface patterns that would otherwise go unnoticed. But without that foundation, AI becomes just another failed promise. It amplifies dysfunction rather than fixing it.

If you want AI-assisted remediation to succeed, you must first make operations predictable. You must first make them **boring.** Table 1-1 provides a Predictable Ops blueprint to evolve your operations From Chaos to Boring.

Table 1-1. Predictable Ops Blueprint

From Chaos to Boring: The Predictable Ops Blueprint		
Maturity Level	**Human Practice**	**AI Assistance**
Level 1—Pain Signals (Chaos)	Log complaints, track downtime, observe frustration points.	Parse tickets, group themes, visualize chronic issues.
Level 2—Documentation	Build runbooks, diagrams, policies, and ticket data.	Summarize procedures, auto-suggest fixes, power chatbots.
Level 3—Stability	Fix recurring issues, enforce process, communicate clearly.	Detect early warning signs, monitor trends, trigger proactive alerts.
Level 4—Efficiency	Remove bad tools, streamline workflows, reduce friction.	Automate steps, recommend optimizations, guide users contextually.
Level 5—Predictable Ops (Boring/Calm)	Review consistently, lead transparently, build team trust.	Deliver insights, scale support, keep operations boring.

This Rule strengthens **Track 1—Operational Trust** by eliminating chaos and making reliability the standard. As we will discover in the coming chapters, this blueprint requires a set of even deeper rules which fill-out the details of the Predictable Ops journey. With this as our starting point, we're ready to move on to how we effectively progress our operations and our team.

Predictability is the bedrock of AI-assisted operations. Without clean processes, documentation, and operational discipline, AI can become yet another failed initiative. As we have stated over and again, the real transformation begins here with fixing the fundamentals.

CHAPTER 1   RULE #1—OPERATIONS SHOULD BE BORING

In the chapters that follow, we'll explore how to use AI tools to enhance accountability, predict delivery risks, and even detect early signs of failure. But none of that works unless your operations are first calm and disciplined.

And yes, boring.

CHAPTER 2

Rule #2 Measure What Matters

KPIs, Metrics, and Machine Learning

Predictability is only reachable when you measure it. The performance data you collect not only shows if you are meeting your goals, it provides information for critical decisions. It is therefore critical to track Key Performance Indicators (KPIs) and performance metrics that give you the information you need to track your journey to Predictability, to highlight what is working, and to expose what is standing in your way.

We measure a lot in our daily lives. We do this so we know what to purchase, what to plan for, how to manage a budget, and how to make countless critical decisions. It's such a natural part of how we function that we often take it for granted. Measurement is survival.

If we didn't have a fuel gauge in our vehicle, would we know if the tank was approaching empty? Maybe. Based on the vehicle's fuel efficiency and how far we've traveled, we could guess. But that's not a reliable (or Predictable) way of doing it. That's intuition, not instrumentation. Instead, we rely on tools and indicators to inform us clearly, especially for decisions that matter.

The same is true for IT operations. **Predictability is only reachable when you measure it, and measure it well.** The performance data you collect not only tells you whether you're meeting your goals; it also feeds the decisions you'll make next.

This is where Artificial Intelligence directly enters the equation. AI thrives on data. The quality of your predictions, anomaly detection, trend analysis, and automated decisions will only ever be as good as the signals you collect. Feed it garbage, and you'll get confident-sounding guesses that lead you in the wrong direction. Feed it clear, contextual, and purposeful measurements, and you gain an intelligent partner that can scale your decision-making capacity.

KPIs and metrics are no longer just dashboards for humans. They're also inputs for machines. If your metrics lack integrity, your AI will too. That makes defining and curating your measurements not just a leadership task, but an **AI governance** responsibility.

Your KPIs and metrics should highlight what is working, expose what's standing in your way, and prepare both you and your systems to respond with intelligence.

This Rule lives in Track 2—**Preparation and Foresight**. Meaningful metrics reveal reality. They're what let you plan ahead, spot risks early, and act with confidence when the numbers change.

CHAPTER 2 RULE #2 MEASURE WHAT MATTERS

Chapter Topics—Rule #2—Measure What Matters

- The KPI Trap
- Metrics vs. KPIs
- Dashboards and True Observability
- Kill the Vanity Dashboard
- AI-Enabled Insights
- Enhancing Insight with Retrieval-Augmented Generation (RAG)
- Root Cause Analysis and Problem Management
- AI Governance—Avoid Blind Faith
- Take a Risk and Prompt the AI
- Chapter Summary

Most teams jump straight to KPIs, assuming they tell the full story. KPIs are **only meaningful when rooted in the right metrics.** You cannot promise predictable outcomes if you're not also monitoring the system health, behaviors, and performance patterns that *feed* those outcomes.

Predictable Ops doesn't just mean tracking KPIs. You must understand the *metrics behind the metrics*. Metrics tell you if the system is healthy. KPIs tell you if the customer experience is sustainable. If you're only tracking KPIs, you're watching the scoreboard and ignoring the game.

AI can supercharge both, but only if the metrics are clean and trustworthy. Before AI can flag a missed SLA or recommend a capacity upgrade, it must have a continuous stream of relevant, structured data. The more consistent your metrics, the more useful your AI becomes.

CHAPTER 2   RULE #2 MEASURE WHAT MATTERS

The KPI Trap

There's an old saying: *"There are lies, damned lies, and then there are statistics."* That's more than just a cynical joke. There's a warning in there as well. The data you collect to track performance, your KPIs, can very easily **lie to you, to your team, and to your customers**.

And in today's world, those lies don't just stop at a dashboard. They can become the fuel for machine-driven decisions. When you feed flawed, vanity-driven, or misaligned KPIs into an AI system, you're not just misleading yourself, you're **teaching your machines to mislead you faster, with more confidence, and at greater scale.**

This is the KPI Trap.

We fall into it when we track what's easy instead of what's meaningful. When we optimize for the metric, rather than the outcome. When we celebrate uptime while ignoring the fact that no one can use the service. And worst of all, when we use KPIs to create the illusion of control rather than a path to improvement. Teams get locked into chasing numbers rather than outcomes. The team culture devolves into gaming the system to achieve the desired numbers.

In an AI-augmented world, this becomes even more dangerous. AI systems don't understand nuance. They optimize toward whatever signals we give them. If those signals are junk, we risk creating beautifully automated, data-driven nonsense.

So before you build dashboards or train algorithms, step back and ask

- Does this KPI reflect reality?
- Does it measure *outcome* or just *activity*?
- If I handed this to an AI system, would it make my operation smarter—or more blind?

Good KPIs guide. Bad KPIs deceive. And when machines are watching, the stakes go way up.

CHAPTER 2   RULE #2 MEASURE WHAT MATTERS

TAKE A RISK—TRUST THE RIGHT METRICS

Not all KPIs are created equal. Some illuminate; others obscure. The risk here is not just in measuring performance but **trusting the wrong measurements**.

When you allow vanity metrics, low-signal data, or poorly defined KPIs to guide your decisions, you're already taking a risk. But when those same metrics become inputs to AI systems, that risk **multiplies exponentially**. AI follows the data and doesn't understand context. If that data is flawed, your systems will confidently drive in the wrong direction.

The brave thing is to throw away blindly trusting your dashboards and challenging them. Sunset your stale KPIs. Redefine the vague ones. Take the risk of measuring what actually matters, not just what looks good in a report.

> **Smart measurement is a calculated risk. Blind trust is a guaranteed failure.**

KPIs vs. Metrics—The Important Distinction

Many organizations treat KPIs and Metrics as interchangeable. This lack of understanding can lead to a massive proliferation of confusing dashboards, tracking vanity numbers that don't drive strategy or continuous improvement, and slows down decision making. Therefore, it is important to understand the distinction.

Metrics are raw measurements—quantitative data about how systems, networks, apps, or processes are performing.

Examples:

- CPU usage
- Memory consumption

- API response times
- Disk latency
- Queue length
- Login errors

Key Performance Indicators (KPIs) are *selected* metrics tied to business or user expectation usually framed around **SLOs/SLAs** and reviewed over time.

Examples:

- Mean Time to Resolution (MTTR)
- Percentage of support tickets resolved within SLA in a month
- Percentage of system uptime over a rolling of 30 days
- Network issue resolution < 60 mins, 90% of the time

Identifying Your KPIs

Establishing your Key Performance Indicators (KPIs) is a deliberate process that has been refined by many operational leaders before you. **You are not inventing from scratch.** Most of the measurements you need already exist in your domain in some form. Your job is to discover them, refine them, and apply them consistently.

Here's how to get started:

- **Know Your Space**
- **Understand Your Customers**
- **Start Small**
- **Standardize Your Tracking Tool**
- **Review on a Standard Cadence**

CHAPTER 2   RULE #2 MEASURE WHAT MATTERS

Know Your Space

You can't measure what you don't understand. Predictable Leaders know the full scope of their operational domain. This includes every critical service, its dependencies, and its expected performance. This means mapping services to outcomes: Which services are customer-facing? Which ones are regulatory or security critical? Which have the biggest revenue impact if they fail?

Take the time, especially if you are new to the role, to document all key areas of your space. Include your team members, customers, and business partners in these conversations of discovery to paint as complete a picture as possible.

Key Areas to Map and Understand:

- **Your Services**

    Document every service you own, from infrastructure to applications. Include descriptions, owners, and key functions.

- **Direct Support Teams**

    Identify the teams directly responsible for maintaining or supporting those services (Ops, DevOps, Security, Networking, etc.).

- **Customers**

    Map which services support external customers, internal business units, or both. Knowing the audience changes the priority.

- **Cross-Team Dependencies**

    Track where your services rely on other teams' systems—and where theirs rely on yours. This prevents surprises during incidents.

- **Criticality Levels**

    Define what "critical" means for your business vs. your industry. A compliance system may be critical for you but optional for others.

- **Regulatory and Security Requirements**

    Flag services subject to regulations (e.g., HIPAA, SOX, GDPR) or heightened security scrutiny.

- **Revenue Impact**

    Estimate the financial hit of a failure. A small outage in one area might be negligible—while another could be catastrophic in minutes.

Don't let your KPIs live in isolation. Every metric you track should tie to a clear operational or business expectation and everyone on your team should know what "good" looks like for that space.

Understand Your Customers

After mapping your customers, Predictable leaders ask themselves one critical question: What do customers really care about even if they struggle to articulate it?

At the core, they care about one thing:

> **What will my experience be like when I engage with IT?**

As a Predictable leader, you must understand those experiences clearly and measure them meaningfully. Only then can you determine whether you're meeting your Service Level Agreements (SLAs) and Service Level Objectives (SLOs).

What are SLAs and SLOs?

These terms are often used interchangeably, but they all serve one purpose:

To define performance expectations and track how predictably you meet them.

Some simple examples:

- Pizza delivered in 30 minutes or less
- Hold time under one minute before an agent answers
- Office internet speed > 100 Mbps
- Overnight delivery of a package
- Shared drives accessible from a corporate laptop

Crude though these may be, they demonstrate a critical truth:

> When you **set an expectation**, customers expect it to be met **Predictably**.

You're not striving for perfection. You're striving for consistency. Depending on the SLA, this might mean meeting the goal 80%, 90%, 99%, or 99.9% of the time.

Example:

> Many platform, infrastructure, and software service providers offer a monthly 99.9% SLA for their uptime/availability. That translates to **no more than 43.2 minutes** of downtime per month.

CHAPTER 2   RULE #2 MEASURE WHAT MATTERS

Start Small

Once you know the breadth of your domain and the expectations of your customers, it can be very seductive to try to measure everything at once. Many leaders will go out of their way to "boil the ocean" in order to identify every possible KPI and associated metric. It is not unusual for the excitement of discovery to encourage rapid deployment at an increasingly accelerated pace. However, now is not the time to overwhelm yourself, the process, or your team.

Begin by tracking the most significant KPIs. These should become clear as you review your space and identify the SLAs and SLOs that are important to your customers. Remember, you need to look at this data through a discerning lens:

- **Metrics** - The telemetry from your various services that give you indications of performance. For example, API response times.

- **SLA/SLO** - Expectations of what that telemetry will tell you. Building on the previous example, the Service Level expectation of your customer could be that the API responds within 25 milliseconds, 99% of the time.

- **KPI** - Identifies how frequently the SLAs are being met—based on the metrics over time—and identifies them as being **important enough to track.**

The next logical question is, "How many KPIs should I start with?" The answer: start with ONE. Tighten down every aspect such as how the data is captured, how it's reported, and how it's acted on (see Standardize Your Tools). When you and your team master measuring one KPI, expanding becomes rinse-and-repeat. That's how you make your KPI process Predictable.

> **⌨ PROMPT THE AI—IDENTIFY YOUR FIRST CRITICAL KPI**

Don't guess which KPI to start with. Test your assumptions with AI.

Upload a simple spreadsheet that lists your core services, the key metrics you already track, and the SLAs/SLOs tied to them.

Then prompt the AI. Begin with setting the context:

"Acting as an IT service management expert,..."

- "Which metrics directly tie to the most visible service impact?"
- "Where does our SLA data show we're closest to missing our customer commitments?"
- "Rank these metrics by potential service delivery risk if they fail."

When you see the patterns, pick the **ONE KPI** that's most likely to move the needle and focus there before you scale.

Standardize Your Tracking Tools

Tool chaos kills Predictability. You don't want 20 dashboards giving you 20 conflicting stories.

Your measurement strategy is only as good as your ability to trust the data and that means consistency. Predictable Leaders don't pull KPIs from scattered tools and spreadsheets. They standardize and aggregate.

Whether you use a single AIOps platform, a trusted data warehouse, or a simple spreadsheet that everyone updates, the goal is the same: make your metrics consumable, consistent, and visible.

This saves your team from spending half their time reconciling conflicting data and lets you spend more time actually improving what the numbers reveal.

There's no one-size-fits-all tool, but Predictable Leaders pick a few trusted, integrated platforms that help them see what matters. Table 2-1, below, highlights some mainstream examples I've used or seen widely adopted in modern Ops environments.

Table 2-1. Common Ops Tools

Platform/Tool	What It's Used For
ServiceNOW	Comprehensive ITSM (ITIL) platform for incident, change, and problem management. Strong CMDB and workflow automation.
Jira Service Management	Agile-focused ticketing, issue tracking, and change control. Popular for DevOps and Ops integration.
PagerDuty	On-call scheduling, real-time incident response, and automated alerting. Helps standardize escalation paths.
Splunk ITSI	AIOps platform for real-time telemetry, correlation, anomaly detection, and root cause analysis.
Datadog/Watchdog	Infrastructure and application monitoring with AI-driven root cause suggestions. Great for cloud-heavy stacks.
BigPanda	Event correlation and noise reduction across multiple monitoring tools. Reduces alert fatigue, standardizes signals.
LogicMonitor	Full-stack observability, especially useful for hybrid cloud environments.
Microsoft Copilot/ ChatGPT	Generative AI for drafting incident updates, standardizing postmortems, or summarizing dashboards.

Your mix will depend on your services, budget, and talent. The real Predictable move is to keep your toolkit simple enough to trust and visible enough that your team can act on the data, not just chase it.

Review on a Standard Cadence

Consistency is key. Metrics are only useful if they're maintained and reviewed on a predictable schedule. Your partners, customers, and employees should know when to expect performance reviews.

If you review KPIs monthly for one quarter, then ignore them the next, you lose trust. One-off reviews break trust. A consistent review rhythm builds accountability. Predictability isn't just in the metric but rather in how **you** show up to communicate it. (*We will discuss Business Reviews in Rule #6—Be a Trusted Partner.*)

Furthermore, the reviews should show how you are trending to the expected SLA, at a minimum. For example, here is a basic IT KPI review for a couple of areas:

KPI	Goal	SLA	Q1 Performance	Trend
Network Issue Resolution	< 60 mins	90%	85%	↓ Down
Password Reset	< 15 mins	90%	95%	↓ Up

This representation might seem like the Network team is struggling and the Service Desk team is knocking it out of the park. Just as we learned in the KPI trap, how data is represented can give us false information. You need to understand HOW you review data is just as critical as the data you choose to review.

Also, don't confuse a calendar check-in with real insight. A Predictable Leader approaches KPI reviews with genuine curiosity: *"Why is this trend happening?", "What does this mean for the customer?", "What hidden factors could be at play?"* Data doesn't reveal its truths by itself. Your job is to dig deeper, question assumptions, and pressure-test what the numbers are really saying.

A predictable review cadence shows you care about consistency. A curious mind shows you care about *accuracy*. You need both. And when you review this data, you need to have action items to resolve them.

A review without action is just a ritual. The meeting feels official, but it doesn't change anything. The point of reviewing KPIs on a standard cadence is to make trends visible *while you still have time to do something about them.*

Every review should end with clear, measurable next steps. If a KPI is trending down, what's the course correction? If it's trending up, what lessons can you apply to other areas?

Over time, this builds real Predictability: you're not just reacting to fires. You're strengthening your services proactively because the data tells you where to focus.

A Predictable Leader doesn't just show up to the meeting. They make the meeting count.

Correlate the Data—Don't Just Collect It

Looking at metrics in isolation hides root causes. Real improvement often comes from seeing the patterns *between* them.

One KPI rarely tells the whole story. Predictable Leaders know how to correlate multiple data points to see what's really driving success or failure.

For example, if your API response time KPI is slipping, look at related metrics: server CPU, traffic spikes, vendor performance, and customer usage patterns.

Correlating the data lets you spot root causes, not just surface symptoms. Sometimes fixing one weak link improves multiple services at once. It's not just measurement but meaningful insight that drives smarter Ops decisions.

You've probably also heard the saying

> "Correlation is not causation."

This cliché carries real weight in operations. The data you collect can mislead you, and AI will confidently accelerate that misinformation if not guided carefully. Predictable Leaders don't trust a single data point or an untested AI correlation. They keep asking, "What else does this affect?" and "What does this pattern really mean for the service and the customer?" That's how you avoid false confidence and fix the real problem **before** it becomes the next incident.

 ## Real-World Example—Invalid Interpretation

At one regional office, end-users began submitting urgent tickets: they couldn't access a critical file share hosted on a specific storage server. Other shares were reachable, but this one was used for daily reporting and was completely offline. The issue was flagged as a potential outage.

Initial logs from the storage system showed signs of failed authentication attempts and intermittent timeouts. The local team immediately escalated. We pulled detailed logs, reviewed recent change controls, and even initiated a diagnostic session with the storage vendor. Nothing appeared obviously broken, but users still couldn't connect.

Meanwhile, productivity was grinding to a halt. Team leads were demanding status updates. The storage system *had* to be the culprit, until someone, almost by accident, checked the endpoint logs on a few of the affected machines.

That's when the real cause was uncovered: a separate support team had silently pushed an update to those users' laptops. That update altered the authentication behavior and broke connectivity to specific file shares. The storage system was fine all along.

In hindsight, all the signs were there but we were too narrowly focused on one domain. Without correlated, cross-domain insight, we chased shadows.

CHAPTER 2 RULE #2 MEASURE WHAT MATTERS

The lesson:
Data doesn't equal truth.
Even smart systems—AI included—can be confidently wrong.
If the signal isn't comprehensive, the conclusions won't be either.

TAKE A RISK—FEED THE FULL PICTURE

Let's reimagine the scenario: What if your AI platform was trained to act, not just observe?

The signal from the storage system looks bad. So the AI starts taking corrective action: rolling back updates, triggering failovers, restarting services. Except…that wasn't the root cause.

The real issue was an unrelated update pushed by another team. The AI wasn't wrong because it's flawed. It was wrong because it had incomplete data.

This is the new risk surface. As we hand over more decision-making to automation, the need to **Measure What Matters** and **correlate across systems** becomes mission-critical. Half the picture is worse than no picture when AI is involved because now it's not just diagnosing, it's acting.

AT MACHINE SPEED.

Take the risk of exposing everything: logs, tickets, change histories, user feedback; even if the data feels noisy or raw. Because the more context your AI sees, the better it performs. And the fewer misfires you'll be cleaning up after.

Dashboards and the Illusion of Control

Many leaders fall into the trap of thinking that if they have enough dashboards, they'll have a clear view into their operations. But more dashboards do not equal better insight. In fact, they often create a false sense of visibility.

CHAPTER 2   RULE #2 MEASURE WHAT MATTERS

Most dashboards reflect the mindset and biases of the person who built them. They may emphasize infrastructure metrics, ticket data, or capacity stats but rarely all of the above in a way that aligns with business or user impact. Others are so high-level or so dense with raw data that it takes a subject matter expert to even interpret what's being shown. In practice, dashboards often generate **noise** rather than **narrative**.

What they typically don't do is surface the "why" behind poor performance or predict the "when" of a coming failure.

What True Observability Looks Like

True Observability is about identifying the *right* patterns, at the *right* time, for the *right* reasons. That means putting metrics into an operational context.

Examples of observable insights:

- Database queries slowing at a consistent time each day
- Internet circuits spiking at the top of each hour (scheduled syncs?)
- CPU load anomalies on a specific server tied to patch jobs or external calls

These are the kinds of signals that surface **predictive patterns**. Patterns that AI tools can detect and highlight *if* you've designed your metrics, logging, and event streams to support them.

Predictable Ops Perspective

In Predictable Ops, dashboards are tools but they are not ***the Truth***. If your observability layer is built around vanity metrics, vague performance graphs, or dashboards with unclear ownership, you've created a mirage, not a map.

CHAPTER 2 RULE #2 MEASURE WHAT MATTERS

The Predictable leader builds a monitoring and observability strategy that

- Tracks meaningful metrics (see earlier section)
- Ties those metrics to service health and user experience
- Enables AI to surface risks before they become failures

Without that foundation, you're just watching pretty charts while your systems break quietly in the background.

TAKE A RISK—KILL THE VANITY DASHBOARD

Dashboards are not sacred. Just because someone spent hours tweaking colors, filters, or Grafana panels doesn't mean the dashboard provides value. In fact, many dashboards are little more than status theater, being pretty, impressive, and completely useless in practice.

If a dashboard doesn't help someone make a decision, take action, or spot a trend before it becomes a problem, then it is merely a distraction.

Taking the risk to question or even remove a cherished dashboard can create tension with the engineer or team that built it. But this isn't about hurt feelings. It's about clarity. The Predictable Leader is willing to say

"This is a beautiful dashboard. What problem does it solve?"

If the answer is vague, redundant, or purely cosmetic, it may be time to deprecate it in favor of dashboards that track real, observable patterns. Your ops environment should not be a wall of screens, it should be a system that helps people make better decisions, faster.

Predictability thrives on signal, not noise. Take the risk. Kill the vanity dashboard.

AI-Enabled Insights: From Data Display to Decision Support

Most IT teams already use dashboards. These have traditionally been the domain of number crunchers and domain experts to analyze. Grafana, Splunk ITSI, Datadog, New Relic, and others offer expansive visualizations that show metrics in real time. But the truth is, dashboards alone are not insights. They're telemetry.

AI turns telemetry into intelligence.

Dashboards Without AI

- Show current system status
- Depend on human attention and interpretation
- Often reflect what one person or team *thinks* is important
- Are static and may miss emerging issues
- Can become overwhelming or irrelevant over time

Dashboards with AI

- Ingest system metrics and logs at scale
- Learn normal behavior across systems and time
- Surface anomalies (e.g., "CPU spikes during off-hours" or "disk IO latency increased after a config change")

- Correlate events across otherwise siloed systems (e.g., "auth failures on App A correlate with DNS latency")
- Predict outages, SLA breaches, or performance degradations before users notice
- Recommend or auto-execute remediation actions (if integrated into AIOps tooling)

 ## How AI Ingests Observability Tools

AI systems (especially AIOps platforms) connect to telemetry pipelines via APIs/REST endpoints to pull dashboards, queries, and alert states. In addition, these tools can integrate direct access to underlying databases and streaming pipelines. Some examples include

- **Grafana/Prometheus:** Exposes time-series metrics
- **Splunk/Splunk ITSI:** Log/event ingestion and correlation
- **AppDynamics/New Relic/Datadog:** Application performance and infrastructure metrics
- **ServiceNow/Jira:** Incident and change records

From there, machine learning engines (or large language models in modern AI platforms) normalize the data into a unified schema. This then enables the engine to accomplish the following:

- Identify outliers
- Recognize repeated patterns of failure
- Detect upstream/downstream dependencies

CHAPTER 2   RULE #2 MEASURE WHAT MATTERS

- Score risk (e.g., "likelihood of a ticket spike today based on recent alerts")

- Summarize health in business-aligned language

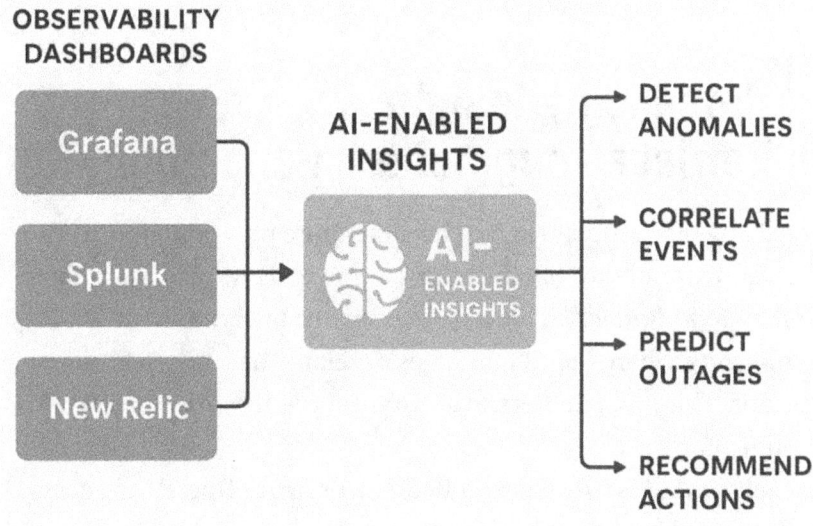

⦿ PROMPT THE AI—TRANSLATE DASHBOARDS INTO INSIGHT

Use prompts like

"Acting as an IT operations observability expert,..."

- "Given this set of Grafana metrics, what anomalies do you detect over the past seven days?"

- "Which dashboards are rarely accessed and may be redundant?"

- "What is the most common root cause of incidents tied to this set of metrics?"

45

CHAPTER 2   RULE #2 MEASURE WHAT MATTERS

- "What time-of-day patterns do you see in system performance?"
- "Can you group related alerts into a single high-level incident?"

Enhancing Insight with Retrieval-Augmented Generation (RAG)

As Large Language Models (LLMs) become more prevalent in enterprise environments, organizations are seeking ways to make them more *operationally aware*. There are legitimate concerns about LLM **hallucinations**, where the AI fabricates unrelated or outright false conclusions. This is where **Retrieval-Augmented Generation (RAG)** comes into play.

RAG allows LLMs like Amazon Bedrock or Azure OpenAI to access internal knowledge sources such as runbooks, performance metrics/KPIs, incident tickets, or system logs, and use that data to improve the quality and accuracy of responses. Rather than relying on a model's pretrained memory, RAG lets you feed information relevant to your organization at the time of the prompt.

In the context of Predictable Ops, this means the data you collect in *Measure What Matters* (your service KPIs, customer satisfaction trends, recurring incidents, compliance thresholds, and so on) becomes a source of organizational intelligence. When structured properly and made accessible through APIs or knowledge indexing, this data can fuel more precise AI interactions.

Example Applications

- Feeding weekly SLA reports into a RAG pipeline, allowing leaders to ask

    "What services are most at risk of breaching SLA this quarter?"

- Connecting known incident patterns to service maps so the model can answer

    "Which systems are most frequently involved in revenue-impacting incidents?"

- Enabling your team leaders to prompt

    "Summarize where customer experience degraded over the past 30 days based on telemetry and complaints."

The power here is not just in asking better questions but rather in giving the AI better data to answer with. RAG turns your telemetry into strategy.

As we continue our transformation into the Age of AI, pairing *measurement discipline* with *retrieval-aware prompting* ensures your operational data doesn't just sit on dashboards. **It becomes the core of your decision-making intelligence.**

 ## AI Governance—Avoid Blind Faith

It's deceptively easy to let the machines think for us. After all, we've done the work in defining KPIs, collecting metrics, feeding logs, building dashboards, and wiring up telemetry for AI to ingest. Surely that means we can now rely on the insights it provides. Haven't we earned that?

Not entirely.

Modern AI tools are exceptionally good at identifying patterns. But unless those patterns are paired with real-world context, they can produce dangerously flawed conclusions. This is where your human judgment comes in.

AI makes mistakes. On the ChatGPT homepage, it plainly states: *"ChatGPT can make mistakes. Check important info."* That's not just legalese, it's the truth. AI-generated insights are powerful, but they are not infallible.

The old axiom *"Trust, but verify"* has never been more critical. Use AI as an advisor, not an oracle. As a Predictable leader, it's your responsibility to validate the insight, not blindly accept it. Otherwise, you risk amplifying the very problems you were trying to solve.

We'll revisit this in Rule #8, where we explore why decisiveness, including the ability to override AI in critical moments, is an essential trait of the Predictable Leader.

PROMPT THE AI—SANITY CHECK THE INSIGHT

AI is great at surfacing trends, predicting risks, and accelerating analysis, but it's not infallible. The Predictable Leader knows when to pause and validate.

Use prompts like

- "How confident are you in this correlation? Could it be coincidental?"
- "What assumptions underscore this insight?"
- "What data is missing that could alter this conclusion?"
- "Could there be another explanation for this trend?"

> **Tip** Ask the AI to provide *alternative interpretations*, even if the insight seems reasonable. Predictability is never about blind faith. Predictability is about due diligence.

Problem Management (aka Fixing What Broke)

Once you've gathered metrics and KPIs, and once your dashboards and ticket systems are surfacing recurring pain points, the next step is obvious but too often skipped: actually fixing what broke.

This is where Problem Management enters the Predictable Ops conversation.

In IT Service Management (ITSM), Problem Management is defined as the process of identifying, documenting, and eliminating the root causes of incidents. In plain terms, it's how you stop things from breaking again.

But here's the catch: many teams still treat Problem Management as an afterthought. They resolve the incident, close the ticket, and move on. Root cause gets pushed to the backlog. Weeks go by. The same issue resurfaces, and the cycle repeats.

Predictable Ops Means Persistent Fixes

You can't have Predictable Ops if your team is stuck in firefighting mode. If the same database alert, login failure, or service slowness shows up week after week, then your operations aren't predictable. They're just stuck in a loop.

Problem Management is the mechanism that breaks that loop.

With the right structure, your team shifts from

- **"What happened this time?"**

to

- **"Why does this keep happening—and how do we eliminate it?"**

 ## AI Accelerates Root Cause—If You Let It

Here's where AI becomes a game changer. You no longer have to sift through a mountain of tickets manually to find trends. Tools like **ChatGPT, CoPilot, or AIOps modules in platforms like Splunk ITSI or ServiceNow** can ingest months of tickets and metrics in seconds and highlight

- Chronic service issues tied to specific infrastructure
- Recurring alerts clustered by user, region, or time of day
- Latency spikes linked to recent code pushes
- Backend failures correlated with third-party vendor downtime

The trick is making sure your data is consistent and structured enough for these tools to make accurate connections. Garbage in, garbage insights.

But when it works? AI can not only spot problems. It can suggest remediations, recommend owners, and even generate a draft Problem Record complete with historical context.

Problem Management As a Trust Multiplier

Fixing recurring problems doesn't just improve uptime. It builds confidence. Your customers stop assuming "this will happen again" and start believing in your ability to solve. Your team gets to work on more strategic tasks instead of chasing the same alerts. And you, as the leader, stop being the escalation path for every blip in the system.

Problem Management is where insight becomes action.

·[AI]· PROMPT THE AI—ACCELERATE ROOT CAUSE

AI-assisted insights can dramatically reduce the time it takes to identify and act on the root cause of recurring issues. Instead of manually reviewing tickets or dashboards, let your AI tools do the heavy lifting.

Use platforms like **ChatGPT**, **CoPilot**, or **your ITSM's built-in AI module** (e.g., **ServiceNow, Splunk ITSI,** and **Dynatrace**) to ingest historical incident data, logs, or service tickets. Then, prompt for correlations and probable causes.

Sample Prompts:

- "Based on this month's tickets, what are the top three recurring issues?"
- "Do you detect any correlation between service outages and time of day?"
- "Can you identify which applications or systems are involved in multiple unresolved incidents?"
- "Highlight any user groups or regions reporting the same types of problems repeatedly."
- "Suggest possible root causes for intermittent slowness on the ERP system every Monday morning."

AI can't fix the problem for you but it can quickly point your team in the right direction and help you make Problem Management a repeatable discipline, not a wishful afterthought.

CHAPTER 2   RULE #2 MEASURE WHAT MATTERS

Chapter Summary—Rule #2—Measure What Matters

This Rule strengthens **Track 2—Preparation and Foresight** by turning raw data into signals you can trust.

Predictability begins with measurement but not all measurements are created equal. In IT operations, **metrics** help you understand what your systems are doing, while **KPIs** help you understand whether your services are delivering. Both are necessary, but they must reflect reality, not just generate reports.

The biggest risk is not a lack of dashboards, but the wrong ones. Leaders often confuse visibility with insight, mistaking broad, unfocused data visualizations for actual observability. True insight comes when your dashboards expose operational friction, not just system performance. If your dashboards don't drive action, it's time to kill the vanity metrics and build something better.

AI raises the stakes. With the right data, AI tools can detect early warning signs, uncover invisible patterns, and accelerate root cause analysis. But fed the wrong data or biased KPIs, AI will just reinforce bad decisions faster. AI-enhanced observability only works when your foundational data is clean, relevant, and contextual.

This is where **Problem Management** becomes key. AI can surface recurring issues that previously went unnoticed, making your remediation work faster and more focused. But it still depends on you to lead. To prioritize the right issues, ask the right questions, and act decisively on what the data reveals.

You're not just measuring. You're shaping the future performance of your team, your services, and your AI.

CHAPTER 3

Rule #3—Develop Your Team

Training Humans for a World of Machines

Too many leaders treat team development as a checkbox: send someone to training, get a certification, and consider the job done. True development is more complex. It requires building trust, setting clear expectations, holding people accountable, creating space for growth, and aligning personal development with business objectives.

As IT operations evolve, so must your team. The coming years will demand more than technical know-how. Your people will need deep data literacy, the ability to work alongside AI, and the skills to translate machine insights into human decisions. This is not optional. If you want Predictable Ops in the age of AI, you must start with a team built for it.

Developing your team is core to **Operational Trust**. A Predictable Leader grows people, not just processes. You build trust through skills, accountability, and a culture that handles change together.

CHAPTER 3   RULE #3—DEVELOP YOUR TEAM

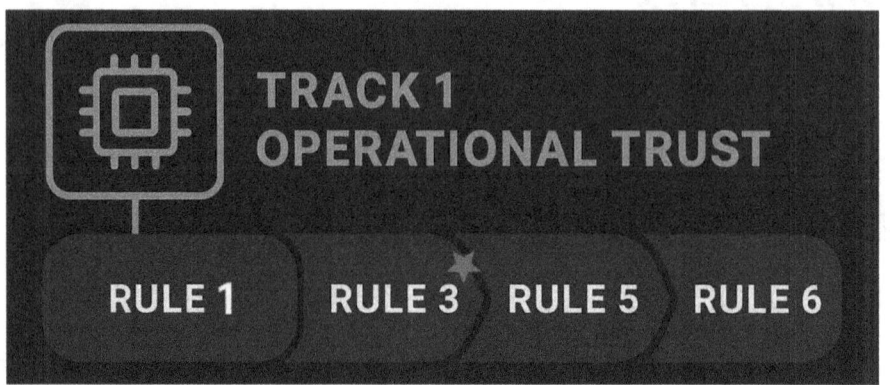

Chapter Topics—Rule #3—Develop Your Team

- Understanding What Your Team Really Is
- Start with Accountability
- Accountability with AI
- Trust and Support Your Team
- Track Capabilities
- Hire for Gaps
- Fear of Change vs. Empowerment
- Take a Risk and Prompt the AI
- Chapter Summary

The Reality Shift

AI and automation are reshaping the work landscape at a frenetic pace. Information Technology tasks previously reserved for humans are increasingly handled by machines. As a result, human work is shifting toward judgment, creativity, and complex problem solving. Teams will fall behind if they don't focus on building new capabilities.

CHAPTER 3   RULE #3—DEVELOP YOUR TEAM

To prepare for this, the Predictable leader views the development of their team holistically.

Understanding What Your "Team" Really Is

Many leaders assume their "team" means only their direct reports and full-time contractors. On the surface, that's true, but it's also incomplete. Before you can dive into what it means to develop your team, Predictable leaders make sure they understand the complete definition of their team, beyond just "standard" resources.

Partners vs. Vendors

Any vendor providing a service to you is more than a transaction. They're an extension of your team. If you treat them as mere salespeople, you'll miss the benefits that come with real partnership. When you approach a vendor with a "team-first" mindset, they're more likely to share insights, flag risks early, and look for ways to help you succeed. That attitude will pay dividends later, especially when it's time to manage costs (Rule #4—*Know What It Costs*) or plan for major changes (Rule #7—*Prepare for the Future*).

Work Partners

Your team doesn't stop at the IT department's edge, either. In a Predictable Ops environment, everyone in your broader business can become a partner in your success, if you build those bridges. Whether it's Finance helping you track spend trends, HR supporting team growth, or business units giving feedback that shapes your roadmap, these relationships expand your influence and amplify your impact.

CHAPTER 3   RULE #3—DEVELOP YOUR TEAM

When you start to see your "team" as an ecosystem, including your people, your vendors, and your business peers, that is when you build resilience. Problems get solved faster. Information flows more freely. Trust scales. When AI tools join the mix, you'll have a stronger foundation to collaborate on what comes next.

> **·AI· PROMPT THE AI—MAP YOUR TRUE TEAM**

Use AI to get a broader picture of who really supports your success and where gaps or blind spots exist.

Sample Prompts:

- *"Based on our vendor spend data, which partners deliver the most value vs. cost?"*

- *"Summarize stakeholder survey feedback: which business units see IT as a partner, and which don't?"*

- *"Who are our top ten external contacts by collaboration frequency and where are the weak spots?"*

- *"What patterns in helpdesk or support tickets suggest that some vendors or work partners are underperforming?"*

Tip   AI won't build trust for you, but it can spotlight overlooked relationships, recurring friction points, or areas where you should invest more effort in making your *whole team* truly Predictable.

CHAPTER 3   RULE #3—DEVELOP YOUR TEAM

Start with Accountability

A former manager once told me something I never forgot: *"Action items without dates are merely suggestions."* It's a truth I've carried throughout my leadership career.

Accountability is often simplified to "doing what you said you'd do." Real accountability is deeper. It's about taking responsibility for outcomes, communicating progress proactively, and owning the impact of your commitments. This becomes especially critical as we enter the AI era, where tasks are accelerated, monitored, and automated, but responsibility still lands squarely on human shoulders.

TAKE A RISK—DRIVE ACCOUNTABILITY

Imagine this scenario:

A team member commits to delivering a report by end of the week. It's 4:00 PM on Friday, and the report still hasn't arrived. Do you

- Ping them to check if they forgot?
- Offer to cover dinner if they need to stay late and finish?
- Assume they'll deliver it eventually and deal with the consequences next week?

Each choice has merit and risk. The first may imply distrust. The second might seem heavy-handed. The third can look like leniency, but it's often just abdication.

The truth is: Predictable leaders know when to nudge, when to push, and when to let someone fail, especially when the stakes are low and the lesson is high. Accountability isn't about control; it's about development. Your job isn't to micromanage delivery. It's to help your team learn what delivering *means*.

CHAPTER 3   RULE #3—DEVELOP YOUR TEAM

As AI systems take on more execution, your human team must elevate their sense of ownership. Accountability doesn't go away in the age of AI. It becomes your differentiator.

·[AI]· PROMPT THE AI—TRACK ACCOUNTABILITY TRENDS

Predictable leaders keep their teams accountable. Not through micromanagement, but by paying attention to patterns. AI tools like ChatGPT can help identify who's following through, who's missing deadlines, and where things might break down.

Upload a task tracker or assignment log and prompt AI:

"Look for patterns in missed deadlines, delayed deliverables, and who's consistently on time. Are there repeat issues by person, task type, or project phase? What stands out?"

Use this data to coach, course correct, or adjust assignments before problems get worse. You're not using AI to see clearly, not to punish. Here's a sample format you might start with:

Form 3.2 – Accountability Tracker (Sample)

Team Member	Task Description	Due Date	Status	Delivered On	Notes
Priya	Update Ops dashboard	Apr 10	Completed	Apr 12	Missed, no comms
Alex	Build SLA metrics tool	Apr 14	Completed	Apr 13	Delivered early
Drew	Review AI model logic	Apr 15	In Progress	—	No update since Apr 10
Stephen	Write incident RCA	Apr 13	Completed	Apr 13	On time

This data can also be stored in a **RAG** source that has been linked via API to your AI tool.

You can then prompt AI to analyze patterns like

- Repeated misses without updates
- On-time delivery by role or task type
- Which tasks stall without check-ins

Predictability doesn't require perfection. It requires visibility and the discipline to act on what you see.

We discuss communicating commitments with customers in **Rule #5**, but from Day 1, establishing this foundation of accountability creates a culture of obligation and expectation to deliver results.

AI Transition Note—The Evolution of Accountability with AI

Holding people accountable used to be based on driving discipline, diligence, and a lot of manual follow-up. Now, AI can take on much of that burden if you're willing to use it wisely.

Let's look at how a typical meeting and its outcomes have evolved:

Past Operations

- Someone takes handwritten or typed notes
- Action items are tracked manually (if at all)
- Owners and dates are emailed out, often inconsistently
- Follow-up relies on memory or a calendar reminder

CHAPTER 3   RULE #3—DEVELOP YOUR TEAM

AI-Enabled Operations

- Tools like **Zoom AI Companion and CoPilot for Teams** transcribe the meeting in real time.
- AI extracts action items and decisions without prompting.
- Assigned owners and dates are pushed into collaboration tools like **Asana, ClickUp,** or **Notion.**
- AI can cross-check workloads and warn about overcommitment.
- Summaries are automatically distributed to attendees.

This is the new bar for operational leadership. AI doesn't replace your leadership—it enhances your visibility, sharpens your follow-up, and makes accountability harder to ignore. Figure 3-1 summarizes this transition to AI.

This is no longer futuristic. It's already here, and if you're not using it, your competitors and peers probably are.

AI won't hold people accountable for you, but it will eliminate the excuses. You don't need to ask, *"What did we say we'd do?"* or *"Who's responsible?"* The AI already knows. Your job is to lead from that truth.

CHAPTER 3   RULE #3—DEVELOP YOUR TEAM

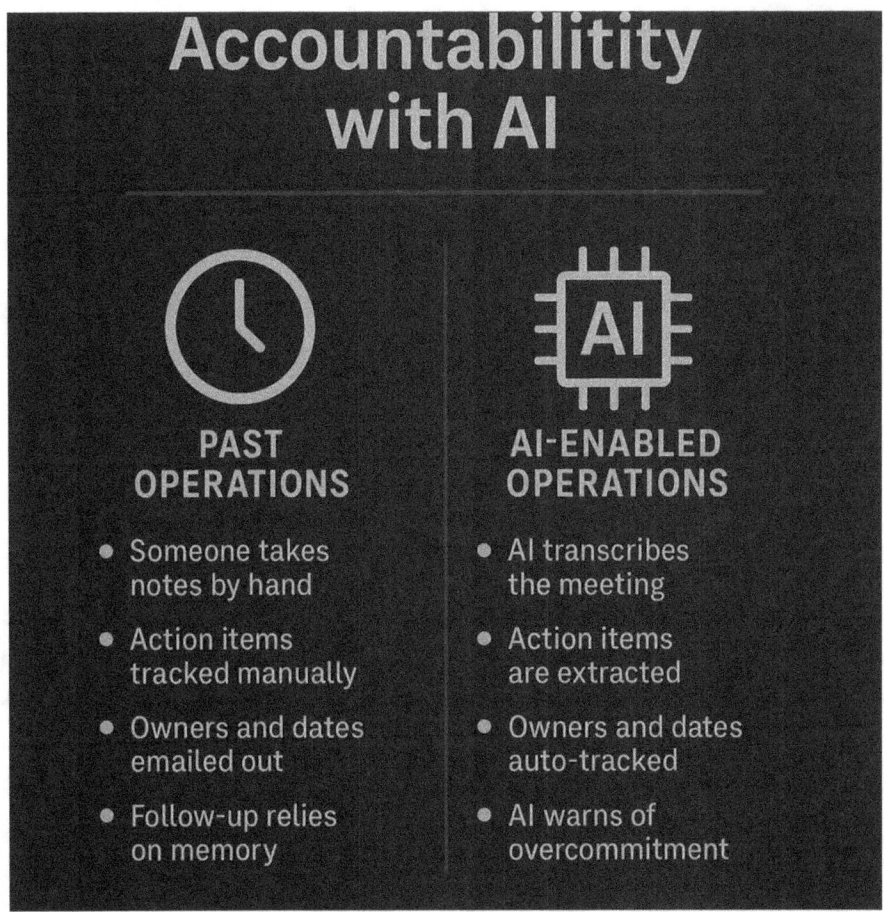

Figure 3-1. Evolution of Accountability

Be Available

Regular check-ins are essential. You can't sit on an island and still expect the team to hit your targets. They need to *know* you.

The Predictable Leader stays present through **consistent, purposeful touch-points**, not by flooding the calendar. "Death by meeting" is real; nobody wants a parade of sync-ups that exist only to *look* like communication. Hold 1:1s, team huddles, or quick async check-ins when they serve a clear purpose. Cancel, shorten, or combine them when they don't.

Your goal isn't airtime; it's **accessibility that builds trust**.

> **Quick metric** – If your team can't get a decision from you within 24 hours, then you're not "available".
>
> **Micro-practice** – End every 1:1 by asking, "What's one blocker I can clear this week?"
>
> **AI angle** – Use a chat assistant to summarize recurring issues across your 1:1 notes so you can spot patterns without adding another meeting.

·[AI]· PROMPT THE AI—UNCOVER HIDDEN HAND-RAISES

Being "available" isn't about clocking more meeting hours—it's about clearing roadblocks fast. You can export last month's chat threads, 1:1 notes, and meeting transcripts, and upload them to generative AI:
Then prompt the AI

- *"From these notes, list any questions or blockers directed at me that have been unanswered for more than 48 hours. Group items by theme, flag urgent items, and suggest the quickest next step I can take."*

AI surfaces the silent stalls your team stopped mentioning out loud. Address them in minutes, and your accessibility goes from a calendar entry to a tangible advantage.

CHAPTER 3   RULE #3—DEVELOP YOUR TEAM

> **TAKE A RISK—PUBLISH YOUR CALENDAR**

Most leaders protect their schedule like root access. Flip it:

- **Expose it.** Make your calendar visible to the whole team. Leave "office-hour" blocks open for anyone to book—no approval loop. *(Many calendar tools allow you to show your available slots without exposing the title or attendees of other meetings, if confidentiality is an issue. Talk to your IT tools team if you have questions.)*
- **Trust the filter.** Let the team decide if an issue is worthy of that slot. You'll be surprised how respectfully they use the time.
- **Trade control for insight.** The risk is losing tight grip on your day; the reward is real-time visibility into blockers you'd otherwise discover too late.

When your team can reach you without ceremony, "availability" stops being a talking point and starts being a superpower.

Trust and Support Your Team

"Delegation" is one of the most overused, under-explained buzzwords in leadership. It's not about pushing tasks off your plate but about showing your team that you trust them enough to step up, take ownership, and grow.

When you *ask* someone to take control of a situation rather than simply *assign* them a task, you empower them with your confidence in their skills. You're saying: *I believe you can handle this.* That belief is contagious.

CHAPTER 3   RULE #3—DEVELOP YOUR TEAM

Nothing grows a team's trust in you faster than showing them you trust them first.

One of the best managers I ever worked for understood this deeply. He knew when to step back and let us solve problems, and he knew when to step in and stand with us when things went sideways. When mistakes happened, he owned them publicly. He shielded the team from unnecessary fallout, then worked with us privately to learn from it. We weren't afraid of being blamed. We were more afraid of letting him down. That's the kind of loyalty real trust creates.

Predictable Ops relies on this culture. When your team knows you'll take the heat, they'll take more initiative. They'll make the tough calls you'd want them to make, even when you're not in the room. They'll innovate because they know that mistakes won't ruin them, and new ideas won't be punished.

Take the Bullets

Fear can drive compliance, but it also kills accountability. People will make mistakes. Your job is to make sure they're not afraid to own them. That means you must be willing to own those mistakes too. Especially when you trusted someone to take a risk in the first place.

Yes, accountability still matters. If someone is consistently incompetent or careless, you deal with it. But when people make honest mistakes while trying to do the right thing, back them up. Take the bullets publicly, coach them privately, and they'll get better. And they'll trust you more each time.

Give Advice

People want to do better. Even the most junior employee lights up when a trusted leader takes the time to teach them how to grow. Giving good advice is a leadership superpower. It shows your team you care about their success, not just their output.

When mistakes happen, you have a choice: rip someone apart for the misstep or use it as a moment of mentorship. The Predictable leader chooses to mentor. Why? Because a culture where mistakes are met with explosions is a culture where no one takes risks, tries new things, or tells you when something goes wrong.

Mentor Their Mistakes

Start by evaluating *why* the mistake happened so your advice actually helps.

> **Technology Failure:** Did a trusted tool break down? Sometimes the blame doesn't belong to your people at all but with a system that needs fixing.
>
> **Process Failure:** Did the person follow the documented procedure, but the outcome still failed? That's a sign your process needs an update, not simply your team.
>
> **Careless Mistake:** Did they cut corners, skip steps, or ignore known best practices? That's where accountability and coaching intersect. Hold them responsible and help them learn.
>
> **Career-Limiting Mistake:** Rare but real. Sometimes a mistake is so severe that trust can't be rebuilt. Here, your Predictable response is to act decisively and fairly, so your team knows you protect the bigger mission.

CHAPTER 3   RULE #3—DEVELOP YOUR TEAM

When you give clear, practical advice, you create a team that wants to learn—not hide their failures. That's how you turn trust into performance, and performance into Predictable Ops.

⟦AI⟧ PROMPT THE AI—SPOT RECURRING FAILURES

Use AI to help you understand where your team needs coaching, not just correction.

Sample Prompts:

- *"Analyze the last six months of incident reports: which types of mistakes happen most often?"*

- *"Do we see patterns where the same person or team repeats an issue?"*

- *"What root causes show up when comparing process failures vs. tool failures?"*

- *"Which mistakes could be avoided with better documentation or training?"*

Tip   Your job is to do more than simply catch errors. You need to fix the systems and habits behind them. AI can spotlight repeat issues faster, so you can focus your advice where it matters most.

CHAPTER 3   RULE #3—DEVELOP YOUR TEAM

Reward Ideas and Improvements

If you want your team to solve problems before they reach you, reward them for doing so. If you want them to bring ideas that make your Ops stronger, recognize and amplify them. Don't just say, "Good job." Share their wins with your peers, your leadership, and your partners. Show that ideation and improvement are part of the culture.

The more you support your team's ideas, big or small, the more they'll trust that they have the freedom to grow, experiment, and find better ways to deliver. And that's the heart of a Predictable team: consistent, resilient, and constantly improving.

TAKE A RISK—LET THEM STRETCH

It's easy to keep the safest people on the hardest work. It's predictable, but it's not scalable. The real risk (and the real payoff) is in letting your up-and-coming team members stretch beyond what they've done before.

Give someone a piece of a tough project. Let them run a meeting you'd normally lead. Let them own the solution when a system goes sideways. Yes, they might stumble. Your willingness to let them try and to stand by them when they do builds real trust.

This risk pays off twice: you grow your team's capabilities, and you create more Predictable Ops because you're not the only one who can fix things when they break.

Use what you learn here to feed directly into how you *track capabilities* and identify growth areas. Trusting your team is the start. Documenting their strengths and gaps is what makes that trust actionable.

67

CHAPTER 3   RULE #3—DEVELOP YOUR TEAM

Track Capabilities

In this Rule, we have discussed how you directly manage your team to develop them. In other words, we have explored how you can be Predictable to them. What we also need to explore is how we understand your team's capabilities, and their capacity to deliver to the business.

As we look back to Rule #1, we discussed how inconsistent service often leads to customer and team frustration. One of the most common reasons behind that inconsistency is simple: **the team leader doesn't truly understand their team's capabilities.**

Refer to **Appendix—Form 3.1: Team Skills Matrix**. Many organizations use some version of this matrix to track three essential aspects of team capability:

- **Individual Resource Skill Capabilities**
- **Team Capabilities in Each Skill Area**
- **Overall Team Capabilities (Averaged)**

You can tailor this matrix to reflect the skills most relevant to your environment—whether technical (e.g., scripting, cloud platforms, application expertise) or "soft" skills like written communication or stakeholder engagement.

In an AI-driven landscape, this becomes even more important. When you begin to adopt AI tools, whether for observability, automation, or predictive analytics, your team's success will depend on **more than technical strength.** They will need **data fluency, systems thinking, and the ability to reason through complex outputs.**

If your team lacks those foundational skills, they won't be able to question the recommendations an AI makes. Worse, they might trust it blindly.

So, when assigning skill scores, be sharply critical. For example, if you think someone might rate a 4 out of 5, but you're only confident they're no less than a 3, **score them a 3.** "Probably" is not "definitely," and false confidence creates fragile teams.

Also, avoid half-points (e.g., 2.5, 3.7). That's not decisive (see Rule #8), and it leads to inflated perceptions of competence. You'll need to know with clarity whether your team is truly ready to support, monitor, and question AI-enabled systems.

⟦AI⟧ PROMPT THE AI

One of the safest and smartest ways to start using AI in IT operations is with **non-real-time analysis**. You don't need to automate decisions to get value. Start by **asking better questions.**

For example, take your **Team Skills Matrix** (see Form 3.1) and feed it into a generative AI tool like ChatGPT or CoPilot. Ask for insights like

"Acting as an IT operations leader,..."

- *"What are the most critical skill gaps on this team?"*
- *"Which skill areas show uneven distribution and may pose a risk to support continuity?"*
- *"Based on these scores, what training priorities should I consider?"*
- *"Are there any patterns or outliers that might require a closer look?"*

This kind of prompt doesn't make decisions *for* you—it makes you **a better decision-maker**. AI isn't just for automation. **It's a thinking partner—if you're willing to ask it good questions.**

CHAPTER 3   RULE #3—DEVELOP YOUR TEAM

Real World Example—Evaluating the Front Line

Many years ago, I tasked one of my Operations leaders with developing a Skills Matrix for our front-line team. This team handled every customer interaction from first contact to final resolution. Their skill set had to cover a lot of ground:

- Products and services
- Common error troubleshooting
- Dashboards and telemetry tools (Splunk ITSI, Grafana)
- Communication tools and escalation tools (Zoom, PagerDuty)
- Written and verbal comms
- Basic troubleshooting steps
- And more…

When we completed the evaluation, three things stood out immediately:

1. Senior team members were strong across the board.
2. Newer resources took far too long to ramp up. Training often took **six months or more**.
3. This created an unhealthy workload: senior staff spent much of their time mentoring and picking up the slack, which slowed everyone down.

As one VP on my steering committee put it: "This is a disaster." They weren't wrong.

We knew we had to solve two big problems: give junior team members a way to level up without draining senior time and cut the onboarding curve dramatically.

The solution was a team "30-Day Boot Camp." My Ops Director and team leads consolidated every bit of documentation we could find: wiki pages, tool references, recorded demos, checklists. We structured it into a daily program. In 30 days (about six work weeks), any new hire could go from zero to confident contributor.

The results were immediate: morale improved, skills ramped up fast, and the Boot Camp became so effective that other IT and Ops teams borrowed it for their onboarding too.

In just three months, our new hire ramp time dropped from six months to six weeks, and our senior staff got back to doing the high-impact work only they could do. That's what it looks like when you build team development into a predictable, repeatable system.

Hire for the Gaps

Developing your team doesn't only mean training the people you already have. It means knowing when you need new capabilities that can't be grown quickly enough in-house.

In the Age of AI, this is especially true. Not every skill can be learned overnight, and not every person will want (or be able) to make the leap. That's why your Skills Matrix must also guide your hiring strategy.

When your roadmap reveals an AI or ML capability you lack, such as a prompt engineering specialist, a data scientist with Ops experience, or a reliability engineer fluent in ML pipelines, don't wait until the pain is unbearable. Hire proactively to fill that gap.

Predictable leaders don't hire reactively. They hire deliberately, with foresight.

This also sends a strong signal to your team: you're investing in their success, not just adding headcount. New skills create new opportunities for everyone to learn, cross-train, and stretch.

CHAPTER 3   RULE #3—DEVELOP YOUR TEAM

TAKE A RISK—HIRE FOR THE GAPS

Developing your team doesn't only mean training the people you already have. It means knowing when you need new capabilities that can't be grown quickly enough in-house.

In the Age of AI, this is especially true. Not every skill can be learned overnight, and not every person will want (or be able) to make the leap. That's why your Skills Matrix must also guide your hiring strategy.

When your roadmap reveals an AI or ML capability you lack—a prompt engineering specialist, a data scientist with Ops experience, or a reliability engineer fluent in ML pipelines—don't wait until the pain is unbearable. Hire proactively to fill that gap.

Predictable leaders avoid hiring reactively and hire deliberately, with foresight.

This also sends a strong signal to your team: you're investing in their success, not just adding headcount. New skills create new opportunities for everyone to learn, cross-train, and stretch.

·[AI]· PROMPT THE AI—SPOT YOUR HIRING GAPS

Once you've mapped your current team's skills, AI can help you spot where the gaps are most critical.

Sample prompts:

- *"Given my current Skills Matrix, what capabilities are underrepresented for AI Ops readiness?"*

CHAPTER 3   RULE #3—DEVELOP YOUR TEAM

- *"Which roles should I prioritize hiring for if I want to build ML support into my Operations team within the next year?"*

- *"How do other teams structure new roles for AI prompt engineering or ML Ops?"*

Remember: AI can help you analyze gaps but the decision to hire ahead is still yours.

 ## Upskilling for AI

Developing your team doesn't stop with traditional technical skills. In the Age of AI, upskilling means giving people the confidence and competence to work *with* intelligent systems, not be replaced by them.

This starts with a shift in your Skills Matrix. It's not enough to track who knows Python, cloud infrastructure, or scripting. You also need to know

- Who understands data literacy such as how to read, question, and interpret AI outputs.

- Who can engineer reliable prompts for LLM tools like ChatGPT, CoPilot, or internal bots.

- Who can help maintain and tune machine learning pipelines for your Ops stack.

- Who is ready to step into new hybrid roles like *AI Ops Engineer* or *SRE with ML specialization*.

Don't make AI literacy optional. Tie it to your accountability framework. Make AI fluency part of each role's expected evolution, the same way you once expected people to learn cloud, virtualization, or CI/CD.

73

CHAPTER 3   RULE #3—DEVELOP YOUR TEAM

Practical Steps to Upskill

- Allocate training time and budget specifically for AI tools that directly impact your Ops.
- Bring in vendors or partners to run workshops on your own real data.
- Give your team a safe "sandbox" to experiment with AI prompts and automation workflows.
- Celebrate early wins to show how AI cuts toil, surfaces new insights, or accelerates root cause analysis.
- Use your Skills Matrix to identify gaps and then document what worked so you can repeat it.
- Combine technical training (AI, data skills) with soft-skill development.
- Run scenario-based exercises where AI plays a decision-support role and humans must interpret results.
- Practice incident response in mixed teams (automation+people).
- Teach teams to spot biases and ask, "Should we automate this?" not just "Can we?"
- Train managers to redesign workflows for human–machine collaboration.

This is what keeps Predictable Ops *relevant* Ops. AI isn't a fantasy that is eventually coming. AI is here. And the Predictable leader ensures the team isn't left behind.

CHAPTER 3   RULE #3—DEVELOP YOUR TEAM

Fear of Change vs. Empowerment

Change always creates anxiety and AI is no different. Some people see it as the ultimate threat: *"Will I lose my job to a machine?"* Others see it as a hype cycle that doesn't apply to them. As a Predictable leader, it's your job to ground your team in the truth: AI isn't here to replace them. Rather, it's here to make them better.

When people understand that AI is a tool, not a verdict, fear transforms into curiosity. The difference is how you lead the conversation. You have to show them

- How AI will *partner* with them and not operate in a black box.
- Where human judgment, ethics, and context still matter more than any model.
- How new skills open new career paths, not dead ends.

This doesn't happen through an email or a lunch-and-learn. It happens through repeated examples: working side by side with AI, seeing it make mistakes, and learning how to override or adjust when needed. Predictability comes when your people feel ***in control*** of the machine and not the other way around.

TAKE A RISK—DEMYSTIFY THE MACHINE

Don't treat AI like an untouchable oracle. Show your team how it works and, most importantly, where it fails. Run live demos. Share prompts that backfire. Discuss ethical risks. Make the tool human. When you demystify the machine, you reduce fear and build trust in how your team will use it.

CHAPTER 3   RULE #3—DEVELOP YOUR TEAM

In Table 3-1, we can see some examples of how traditional IT roles can map to the world of AI. Not only are we preparing our Predictable Ops for the Age of AI transition, we are building a transition for our team as well.

Table 3-1. *Skills Evolution Table—From Traditional IT to AI-Enabled Roles*

Traditional IT Skill	Example Role Today	How It Evolves with AI	Example New Role
Scripting and Automation	Systems Engineer	Prompt engineering for automation workflows	AI Ops Engineer
Data Analysis	Business Analyst	ML model tuning, validating AI insights	ML Ops Analyst
Monitoring and Incident Response	NOC Analyst	AI-enabled anomaly detection and root cause analysis	Reliability Engineer with ML
Runbook Development	ITIL Process Manager	Training AI agents with well-structured inputs	AI Support Agent Designer
Vendor Management	IT Vendor Manager	Analyzing spend and vendor performance with AI	AI Vendor Insights Lead
DevOps/CI-CD	DevOps Engineer	Integrating AI testing and feedback loops	AI Pipeline Engineer

This table may also be referenced in the Appendix as Table C-3.

Chapter Summary—Rule #3—Develop Your Team

A **Predictable Leader** does more than manage tasks—they **grow people, expand capability, and clear road-blocks before they stall momentum**. In the Age of AI, this means building a culture where **accountability, trust, and continuous improvement** feel routine, not aspirational.

1. **Set the bar and then stand beside it.** Make ownership explicit, but stay available. Publish your calendar, keep purposeful 1:1s, and use AI to surface unmet "hand-raises" so blockers never linger unseen.

2. **Balance edge and empathy.** Hold firm on results while mentoring mistakes, rewarding experiments, and replacing fear with empowerment.

3. **Track skills with brutal honesty.** Map today's strengths, spotlight gaps early, and turn AI insights into concrete up-skilling plans.

4. **Hire ahead of the curve.** When the gap is too wide to close in time, bring in fresh talent that lifts the whole bench.

5. **Expand the definition of "team."** Vendors, partners, even AI copilots are part of your delivery chain, so treat them like contributors, not conveniences.

6. **Make AI a force-multiplier, not a threat.** Teach data literacy, prompt engineering, and ML-ops basics so the team sees AI as leverage for relevance rather than a reason to worry. Position AI as an amplifier, not a replacement.

7. **Reward curiosity.** Encourage experimentation and make your environment a safe place for employees to admit their struggles, continuously learn, and grow with confidence.

Do this well and you don't just develop people. You forge **Predictable Ops** that thrive, evolve, and lead, no matter how fast technology turns.

CHAPTER 4

Rule #4—Know What It Costs

The Economics of IT Services

Surprisingly, many leaders don't have the slightest clue how much it actually costs to deliver their services. This creates the illusion, or worse, the delusion, that those services are somehow "free." In traditional IT, in the Cloud, and now with AI platforms, cost ignorance isn't just a gap but a leadership failure.

AI has the potential to model your costs more accurately (and, yes, predictively), but only if you've already done the work of capturing those costs in the first place.

Cost is more than a budget line. Every outage, every integration, every vendor decision carries a cost. And while many leaders claim to "own their budget," very few can account for where every dollar goes or explain why costs fluctuate quarter to quarter.

That's because cost transparency in IT remains fragmented. The financial tools used by procurement and finance, like Oracle Financials, Adaptive, and NetSuite, are friendly to operational leaders but not as timely as needed. Costs come in late. They're buried in line items. And even when you have access, deciphering them requires manual work, endless vendor calls, and hours of spreadsheeting.

CHAPTER 4   RULE #4—KNOW WHAT IT COSTS

As of today, **AI isn't solving this problem for us** (at least, not yet!). While AIOps platforms can forecast trends in utilization or ticket volume, they don't always pull from your general ledger or contracts database. The so-called "AI for finance" platforms are mostly focused on enterprise analytics and CFO dashboards, not day-to-day ops decisions.

This Rule is pure Track 2—**Preparation and Foresight**. You can't plan the future or protect trust if you don't know what it really costs to get there.

Chapter Topics—Rule #4—Know What It Costs

- The Predictable Path Forward
- Costs Always Increase
- Beware False Savings—The Assumption Failure
- Vendor Relationships
- Understand Your Contracts
- Return On Investment (ROI)
- Forecasting Costs with AIOps, Analytics, and Generative AI
- Take a Risk and Prompt the AI
- Chapter Summary

CHAPTER 4   RULE #4—KNOW WHAT IT COSTS

The Predictable Path Forward

A Predictable Leader never waits for Finance to say the budget is blown. They keep a rolling view of usage, contracts, license creep, and planned growth. That's your Early Warning System built on signals, not gut feelings.

- **Operational familiarity with your IT spend**

    You must understand your vendors, contracts, SKUs, renewals, and variable costs. AI can help highlight anomalies *once you have **the data**,* but the discipline of owning the inputs still belongs to you.

- **A working relationship with finance**

    Insights are useless if you're cut out of the budgeting conversation. Use your modeling to support budget justification, but build the trust that earns you a seat at the table.

- **AI-assisted cost tracking (when possible)**

    Some vendors are starting to open APIs to query spend. AI agents can help you

    - Summarize line-item changes over time
    - Compare contract values to actual usage (SaaS, cloud, etc.)
    - Identify outliers in month-to-month billing
    - Draft "what if" scenarios using operational trend data

CHAPTER 4   RULE #4—KNOW WHAT IT COSTS

> ## TAKE A RISK—EXPOSE THE REAL COST
>
> One of the boldest moves an IT leader can make is to **surface what things actually cost** and then be willing to talk about it. Not just with Finance. With your peers, your team, and your business partners.
>
> Why is that a risk?
>
> Because real numbers kill assumptions.
>
> That tool your team insists is "mission critical" but costs six figures and gets used by five people? That vendor your exec sponsor loves, but delivers marginal value? That cloud service with unpredictable spikes every month?
>
> When you expose those realities, you'll invite scrutiny. You'll invite debate. But you'll also build **trust**.
>
> Transparency lets you move from defensive to strategic:
>
> - "Here's what this service costs per user."
> - "Here's where we're overspending based on usage."
> - "Here's how AI insights helped us reduce costs on X."
>
> The risk isn't in revealing the numbers.
>
> The real risk is in not knowing them.

I once had a network operations leader who prided himself on knowing exactly how much his services cost the company each year: *"to the penny,"* he'd say. He maintained zero budget surprises for himself, the business, or his customers. He had become, at least when it came to expenses, completely Predictable.

This level of cost clarity is complicated to reach in practice. It requires an honest, detailed understanding of where your money goes and how those costs evolve. At a baseline, this means tracking areas such as

CHAPTER 4   RULE #4—KNOW WHAT IT COSTS

- **Compensation and Benefits** – Often the largest line item. Knowing your fully loaded headcount costs (salaries, benefits, and taxes) is essential for service cost transparency.

- **Operational Expenses**
  - Tools licenses, support contracts, and SaaS or PaaS fees
  - Facilities costs, data centers, and utilities
  - Leased network circuits or other recurring OPEX

- **Capital Expenditures**
  - Hardware refresh cycles
  - Project-driven investments
  - Capacity growth

- **Year-over-Year Increases**
  - The hidden risk of *cost bloat* including unmonitored creep in licensing tiers, underutilized tools, or vendor price escalations.

The Predictable Leader makes these costs visible for yourself, and for the partners and stakeholders who depend on your services to run efficiently.

This visibility is only the start. With this baseline in place, you're ready to tap AI's power to track trends, spot anomalies, and surface hidden costs that manual reviews often miss. In the age of AI, your cost transparency is about building a system that continuously forecasts, alerts, and optimizes how you spend. Even small leaks, if unchecked, can turn predictable costs into runaway chaos.

We'll explore how to *Prompt the AI* for spend trends, test assumptions, and pressure-test your budget models.

CHAPTER 4   RULE #4—KNOW WHAT IT COSTS

Budget Accountability Is Team Accountability

No single leader can carry every line item in their head, and therefore every leader must build a team that knows what it costs to do what they do.

A Predictable Leader doesn't guard the budget like a secret. Everyone who makes decisions such as engineers, project managers, and vendor managers should understand the costs they influence and the real risks that can appear when spending drifts.

When your team knows how their work ties to actual spend, they're more likely to raise the flag early. Are license counts creeping up faster than usage trends? Did a "temporary" service become permanent with no funding plan? Are we duplicating spend across teams because no one's connecting the dots? These are the small cost traps that snowball when you rely on the budget review cycle alone.

This is why cost accountability ties directly to team development. If your leads don't know what knobs they can turn and the early signals to watch for, you'll end up firefighting spend problems later. Teach your people how to spot spend risk just like they spot operational risk. Show them how to use AI prompts and simple trend reports to test assumptions before the surprises occur.

When your team sees cost forecasting as part of their job, you build Predictable Ops that scale with a transparent budget and heightened team credibility.

Costs Always Increase

Costs are never static. Accept this as an operational axiom: prices will go up, sometimes in small, steady increments, sometimes in jarring leaps. If you ignore this, you'll always be playing defense when budgets balloon, vendor renewals spike, or new initiatives pull dollars you didn't plan for.

Once you embrace this truth, you can plan around it. You can even use it to your advantage. Predictable leaders don't pretend they can freeze spend; they build the discipline to make cost *increases* visible, explainable, and manageable.

So how do you make costs more Predictable when they're guaranteed to grow? It starts with a few critical habits and choices:

- **Multi-Year Agreements**

  Lock in pricing wherever possible. A well-negotiated multi-year deal can buffer you against sudden market changes and vendor whims. But don't blindly accept auto-renewals—review the value year over year.

- **Vendor Relationships**

  Treat your vendors like strategic partners, not just order-takers. When you're open about your Predictable Ops goals, you'll often find they can help you uncover hidden discounts, unused licensing, or contract levers that smooth out cost jumps.

- **Economies of Scale**

  Understand your growth curve. Consolidate redundant tools, standardize where possible, and buy capacity wisely. Adding new users or services doesn't always need to scale costs linearly—look for efficiencies that offset increases.

- **Operational Frugality**

  Teach your team to think like owners. If you've ever been shocked by a cloud bill or surprise license overages, you know the pain. Create clear guardrails for usage, monitor for waste, and embed cost awareness in every technical decision.

CHAPTER 4   RULE #4—KNOW WHAT IT COSTS

The goal isn't to stop costs from rising but rather to make those rises predictable enough that they don't become a crisis.

When your CFO or business partners ask, "Why did this go up?" you should have the answer, supported by clear numbers, clear agreements, and a clear plan for what comes next.

·[AI]· PROMPT THE AI—FORECAST SPEND TRENDS

Once your billing data is exported, or you've structured spend by vendor or category

"Analyzing this as an IT budget manager,…"

- "Based on this export, which vendors show the largest increases over the past three quarters?"
- "Are there services we are consistently underutilizing based on cost vs. usage?"
- "What are my top five cost centers for IT support vs. infrastructure vs. licenses?"
- *"Where might we see cost spikes if we grow headcount by 20% next year?"*
- *"What costs could we negotiate down based on multi-year trends?"*

Remember: AI won't give you access to your financial system. Once the data is out, it can synthesize, summarize, and even visualize insights far faster than traditional spreadsheet crunching.

Real World Example: A Cloud Reality Check

Several years ago, we were given a clear executive mandate: investigate a full business continuity and disaster recovery site in the Cloud for a major service running in our on-premise data centers. The long-term vision was that this BC/DR setup would pave the way to migrate all services to cloud platforms eventually.

A large Tiger Team was formed, working closely with our chosen Cloud vendor. And since AI tools weren't mainstream yet, our entire analysis was raw, manual comparison: physical IOPS to Cloud IOPS, physical CPU cores to virtual instances, on-prem load balancers to cloud ELBs and ALBs.

When the grunt work was done, the truth was clear: this service simply wasn't cloud-ready. A pure "lift-and-shift" copy for BC/DR would have been massively cost-prohibitive. In fact, more expensive than the risk it was meant to protect against.

Because we did the modeling upfront, leadership had the facts to pivot. They could see that moving everything to the Cloud would only make sense if we first redesigned those services to be cloud-native. The strategy was to start small and focus on critical, high-ROI services that actually benefited from a Cloud architecture.

If we'd just proceeded on the mandate alone, we'd have built a wildly over-engineered DR site that drained money with no real operational gain. The analysis (though tedious at the time) gave us the **Predictable Ops** clarity to do it right, not just do it fast.

The Lesson: Good cost modeling protects your credibility while protecting your budget. The Predictable Leader knows that every major platform decision is a cost decision in disguise.

CHAPTER 4   RULE #4—KNOW WHAT IT COSTS

> **⋅AI⋅ PROMPT THE AI—STRESS-TEST YOUR CLOUD MIGRATION**

Today, you don't have to run massive manual comparisons alone. Generative AI can help you stress-test migration plans, model usage scenarios, and surface where your services still aren't Cloud-ready.

Sample Prompts:

- *"Analyze these on-prem server specs and workload profiles. What would equivalent Cloud costs look like?"*

- *"Compare our physical IOPS to expected Cloud IOPS. Where might we overprovision?"*

- *"Which services in this plan need redesign to be cloud-native. What would that save us over three years?"*

- *"Show me worst-case vs. best-case cost scenarios if we move this service as-is versus redesigning it first."*

Real World Example—Licensing Increase

Not too long ago, we saw an early sign of a serious budget risk with our software licensing and support costs. Our vendor announced new per-core licensing models with projected cost increases of up to 125%. Even worse, they were requiring three-year agreements, locking us into a spending trajectory that our existing forecast didn't cover.

Our renewal window was Q3, which gave us just a few months to get ahead of the spike. We worked closely with our Value-Added Reseller and the vendor directly to map every piece of our virtualization footprint, consolidate workloads, and model the impact of every license and support scenario.

We used our real utilization trends and scenario stress-testing to back up our plan. By the time the renewal date hit, we didn't see a 125% increase, we negotiated it down to a *six-figure annual reduction* from our original forecast.

If we'd trusted the vendor's initial projections, or waited too long to challenge them, that single line item would have eaten a big chunk of our capacity for growth. That's Predictable Ops in action: *see the cost curve coming, shape it before it shapes you.*

Beware False Savings—The Assumption Failure

One of the most costly mistakes an IT leader can make is to assume savings that never materialize. If you're not careful, the promise of "cost efficiency" can end up doing the exact opposite, locking you into spend that's higher and harder to untangle.

Consider the early rush to Cloud infrastructure. Many leaders saw the savings on paper: "No more expensive datacenter rent, no more racks to maintain, no more on-prem power and cooling costs." But instead of re-architecting for Cloud-native efficiency, they simply lifted and shifted legacy workloads as-is.

What happened? The costs didn't just stay the same: they ***exploded***.

Idle resources spun up 24/7. Over-provisioned VMs drained budgets. Unmonitored storage ballooned. And the dream of predictable spend turned into unpredictable spikes that hit the bottom line without warning.

The lesson? *You can't wish your way into savings.*

You have to plan for them, measure them, and test your assumptions relentlessly.

CHAPTER 4   RULE #4—KNOW WHAT IT COSTS

Use AI to Test These Assumptions Faster

- Will the new architecture really cost less once it's running at scale?
- Are there hidden fees, premium tiers, or data transfer costs you're ignoring?
- What happens if your usage pattern changes six months from now?

Predictable leaders don't fall for the illusion of "cheap."

They know the real cost comes from poor planning, lazy analysis, or vendor promises that sound too good to be true.

Every time you see "potential savings," ask the follow-up:

Where's the trade-off?

How do we prove it?

How do we keep it Predictable?

> **·AI· PROMPT THE AI—PRESSURE TEST THE SAVINGS**

When you're planning for new spend or "expected savings," don't just take the pitch at face value. Use AI to surface hidden costs and test your assumptions.

Sample Prompts:

- *"Based on this proposal, where could hidden fees or variable costs appear?"*
- *"What usage patterns might push us into a higher spend tier?"*
- *"What comparable case studies suggest we could exceed budget?"*

- *"How does this new model compare to our historical cost trends?"*

Tip AI won't replace real scenario modeling, but it can generate questions you might miss in the rush to "save money." Think of it as your reality-check before you sign.

Vendor Relationships

In Rule #3, we explored how your team is bigger than your payroll. Predictable leaders know that your vendors and Value Added Resellers (VARs) are an extension of your operational ecosystem. Treat vendors and VARs like partners, not just order-takers, and they will reward you with insights that go far beyond a contract.

A trusted vendor relationship does more than deliver products. It gives you **forewarning** on cost increases, access to new bundles that could help you consolidate spend, and early signals about emerging technologies that align with your roadmap. Good vendors will proactively show you how to get more from what you already pay for, not just upsell you into more spend.

When tough budget conversations happen as they always do, strong vendor relationships can protect you from surprises. You'll know what's coming, when a renewal bump is likely, and where you have room to negotiate.

Furthermore, a trusted partner will proactively keep you informed and invested in the relationship. That is, **IF** you put in the time to nurture it.

CHAPTER 4 RULE #4—KNOW WHAT IT COSTS

Depending on your level of spend and the strength of your partnership, they might arrange any of the following:

- **On-Site Sync-Ups:** The most common—your account rep makes a house call at your office, or takes you out for a meal to talk business. These are great for day-to-day updates, small renewals, and early issue spotting.

- **Formal Business Reviews:** These can be on-site, virtual, or a hybrid but usually include multiple account managers, technical leads, and customer success leaders. Good reviews are more strategic than a sales pitch: they surface trends in spend, highlight opportunities to optimize, and make sure there are no surprises in the renewal cycle.

- **Executive Briefings:** If the relationship is mature and your spend is significant, the vendor might invite you to their Executive Briefing Center. These sessions go beyond today's contract; they cover the relationship's evolution, possible joint strategic initiatives, and a peek into the vendor's product roadmap, thus giving you a head start on planning.

These touchpoints mark the shift from vendor-customer to real partnership. Predictable Leaders know that investing in these relationships helps you see new opportunities, manage cost surprises, and keep your partners accountable for the value they promise.

When you build Predictable Ops, you build trust externally. You keep your vendor relationships clear, honest, and mutually beneficial. Over time, this ecosystem of partners makes your entire financial journey more stable, transparent, and most importantly—Predictable.

CHAPTER 4   RULE #4—KNOW WHAT IT COSTS

TAKE A RISK—BUILD THE RELATIONSHIP BEFORE THE DEAL

Anyone can negotiate after the costs hit the ledger. The real opportunity is to build trust with your vendors long before a renewal or cost increase shows up. Be transparent about your priorities, your Predictable Ops philosophy, and where you need their insight—not just their products.

When you share your roadmap early, the best vendors become true partners. They'll alert you to price hikes, hidden fees, and cost-saving bundles you'd never find on your own. The risk is investing the time to nurture these relationships. It takes effort, and it's not always comfortable, but the payoff is massive: no surprises, no panic renewals, and far fewer "gotchas" down the road.

⋅[AI]⋅ PROMPT THE AI—ANALYZE VENDOR SPEND

Use AI to see where your vendor spend could be optimized and where risks might hide.

Sample Prompts:

- *"Based on our spend history, which vendors show the biggest cost fluctuations over the past 12 months?"*

- *"Which renewals or license tiers are we underutilizing or paying for twice?"*

- *"What does our vendor mix look like compared to industry benchmarks?"*

- *"Where could bundling or renegotiation save us money in the next fiscal year?"*

CHAPTER 4   RULE #4—KNOW WHAT IT COSTS

Understand Your Contracts

Contractual terms and conditions are hidden specters that many leaders fail to recognize or fully grasp. The Predictable Leader doesn't need to be a lawyer, but they absolutely need to understand how their contracts affect their company's future. Contracts impact not only the financial bottom line, but can either enable or restrict future growth decisions. Understanding how your agreements influence budget and strategy is critical to being Predictable.

Predictable Leaders review contracts not just at renewal time, but as part of their ongoing planning and strategy cycle. Ask yourself: *What will this vendor relationship look like two years from now? What are we locked into? What happens if we need to exit or pivot?*

"Costs" aren't just financial when it comes to contracts. Beyond what you pay for a service or product, the fine print can limit what you're allowed to do, or even bury costs you won't see until it's too late.

Here are a few examples of hidden costs and restrictions that show up more often than you think:

- **Noncompete Clauses**: Restrict your company from working with competing vendors—sometimes across your **entire business**. These clauses can quietly confine your strategic options for years.

- **Auto-Renewal Traps**: Multiyear agreements that autorenew with a short cancellation window (e.g., 30 days before expiration). Miss that window, and you're locked in again, often at a higher rate.

- **Usage Caps and Overages**: Contracts with vague usage definitions that penalize you for growth. Go over the threshold, and you face surprise overage fees or throttled service.

- **Limited Liability**: The vendor limits their responsibility for service outages or even negligence, leaving your business with no recourse for lost revenue.

- **Data Ownership Clauses**: Agreements where the vendor keeps ownership of metadata or analytics generated on their platform, even when it's your operations that generate the data.

- **Integration Penalties**: Limits or fees on API access that quietly punish you for trying to automate or integrate their product into your stack.

- **Unilateral Price Increases**: Language that allows the vendor to raise prices annually, either by a set percentage or based on CPI, without renegotiation.

Predictable Leaders bring procurement, legal, and finance into the conversation early. They build strong vendor relationships, but they don't treat contracts as boilerplate. Instead, they treat them as strategic tools, ones that can either support or sabotage your ability to operate with control.

TAKE A RISK—COMPETING QUOTES

The Predictable Leader doesn't just shuffle vendor quotes through the system or negotiate half-heartedly with a single provider. Strong relationships with vendors and VARs are important, but those relationships still need guardrails.

One way to reinforce fiscal discipline is to implement a policy that requires **competing quotes** for any new contract or renewal exceeding a specific total contract value (TCV). In past organizations, I've set this threshold at $100,000, but you'll need to set a number that fits your environment. Make it high enough to avoid overwhelming your procurement process, but low enough to capture meaningful spend.

CHAPTER 4   RULE #4—KNOW WHAT IT COSTS

Yes, this can be risky. Requesting competing quotes can strain an otherwise strong vendor relationship. The Predictable Leader knows that loyalty doesn't mean complacency. It's your responsibility to keep vendors engaged and not overly comfortable. Easy contracts and mindless renewals are the enemy of financial clarity.

The savings you uncover through disciplined procurement add up, and they create room for reinvestment in innovation, security, or team development.

Take a risk. Get the right deal at the right price, regardless of the vendor.

Return on Investment (ROI)

Calculating ROI, **the time it takes for an investment to pay for itself**, is as much art as it is science. The Predictable Leader applies it to every major expense: contracts, technology consolidation, transformation projects, and beyond.

Spending money without understanding how quickly the company benefits is operating in blind-faith, not Predictability.

For example, migrating to a new tool might seem to be the right plan. The vendor has sold you on the annual cost savings, engineers are pushing for the change, and all seems to be a winning combination. Until, that is, you look at things holistically and through the lens of Return On Investment.

Key ROI Factors for IT Investment

- **Total Contract Savings** - Annual savings or cost for the new tool or consolidation.
- **Implementation Costs** - Project related expenses for the transformation.

- **Productivity Impact** - Loss or gain in team efficiency during and post-transition.

- **Support Costs** - Training or additional staffing costs, or reduction in support costs.

- **End User Training** - Time and expense to ramp up the user base.

When the Predictable Leader considers just these simple items, a basic Cost-Benefit analysis can be calculated resulting in a RO estimate.

Working from the previous example of tool consolidation, let's examine some simple numbers:

Factor	Year 1 Cost/Savings
Total Contract Savings	$100,000/year (savings)
Implementation Costs	$75,000
Productivity Impact	$20,000 loss
Support Costs	$10,000
End-User Training	$30,000

Total Year 1 Cost: $135,000
Annual Savings: $100,000

ROI = ~**16 months** before the savings outweigh the upfront investment.

Many organizations target 12, 18, 24, and 36 month ROI estimations in their decision-making process. Whether such a cost in time, training, and political capital is worth it will depend upon the partnerships you build in the business (Rule #6).

Predictable Leader takeaway: A reduction in a contract cost is not savings until you've calculated the return.

CHAPTER 4   RULE #4—KNOW WHAT IT COSTS

Forecasting Costs with AIOps, Analytics, and Generative AI

As of today, no single AI tool will pull every line from your general ledger and vendor contracts to hand you the perfect operational spend forecast. AI can still help you get there faster if you know how to bridge your tools.

AIOps platforms, like **Splunk ITSI** or **ServiceNOW**, already give you real-time trends: utilization spikes, ticket volumes, and unexpected patterns in capacity. These aren't just support stats, they're early warnings that your cost curves are about to shift.

AI analytics tools, whether that's an IBM Watson model or an enterprise BI tool with an AI layer, can surface usage anomalies and tie them back to spend drivers. They won't call your vendor for you, but they'll tell you which services are trending hot *before* the bill surprises you.

Generative AI, like **CoPilot** or **ChatGPT**, is the glue. It can't generate a new contract, but it can turn raw AIOps data into usable "what if" scenarios. For example:

- *"If utilization continues at this rate, what's our expected spend in the next three quarters?"*
- *"If we consolidate workloads, what would the license footprint look like?"*
- *"Where might we run into hidden support fees that aren't obvious in our main budget?"*

Used together, these tools help Predictable Ops leaders do what spreadsheets and stale dashboards can't: **pressure-test assumptions before they turn into cost overruns.**

CHAPTER 4   RULE #4—KNOW WHAT IT COSTS

🔲 PROMPT THE AI—FORECAST SPEND TRENDS

Predictable Ops leaders look at more than just last month's invoice. They also ask AI to stress-test the future before it surprises them. Use your AIOps trends, ticket data, and contract assumptions to build realistic, actionable scenarios you can share with finance.

Try this:

Prompt:

"Given our last 12 months of utilization, ticket volume, and capacity trends from Splunk ITSI and ServiceNOW, forecast our operational spend for the next three quarters.

Include:

- **Baseline projection:** *If current trends continue.*

- **Upside scenario:** *If usage spikes by 20% or we accelerate a planned project.*

- **Downside scenario:** *If we delay upgrades, consolidate workloads, or decommission legacy services.*

- **Hidden cost risks:** *Identify support costs, license overages, or non-obvious fees that might not appear in our general ledger yet.*

- **External triggers:** *Note any vendor announcements or regulatory changes that could affect our assumptions.*

- **Narrative summary:** *Draft a short paragraph for my next QBR slide to explain these risks in plain English.*

Tools like CoPilot or ChatGPT are great at narrating complexity. Once you have the AIOps data from Splunk or ServiceNOW, paste it in then ask for alternative spend scenarios, risks, and fallback options. You're responsibly clarifying the assumptions, before those assumptions cost you.

TAKE A RISK—PRESSURE TEST THE SAVINGS, AGAIN

A vendor will always tell you they're saving you money—especially when they're changing how they price or license your services. Don't just nod and sign. Use your AI-generated scenarios and vendor spend analysis to stress-test every claim.

Ask the uncomfortable questions:

- *"What if usage spikes? How does this model still hold?"*
- *"Where's the hidden cost if we grow faster than expected?"*
- *"What's the cost to exit or renegotiate midstream?"*

When you push back, you find out whether the partnership is truly collaborative or just convenient for them.

The Predictable Leader doesn't get blindsided at renewal time. They see the cost curve coming and shape it before it hits.

Chapter Summary—Rule #4—Know What It Costs

This Rule strengthens **Track 2—Preparation and Foresight** by putting cost awareness at the center of every smart decision.

A Predictable Leader knows that cost surprises are the fastest way to lose trust with the business, partners, and customers. Budget forecasting isn't just plugging numbers into last year's spreadsheet; it means seeing the real drivers of spend before they become problems, from platform usage and ticket spikes to hidden vendor risks, over-engineered systems, or services that aren't built for the platforms they run on.

AI tools like AIOps, analytics, and generative modeling can surface trends and test your assumptions fast. However, they're only as useful as your willingness to ask the uncomfortable questions. Vendors will always promise savings; it's your job to pressure test those stories before they become a six-figure regret.

And this discipline can't live with you alone. In Predictable Ops, every team lead must know what spend they influence and what early signals matter most. The team that understands cost and risk is the team that earns trust because **they don't get surprised**. They see the cost curve before it bends, shape it before it breaks the budget, and prove that their numbers, plans, and promises are worth betting on.

CHAPTER 5

Rule #5—Communication Is Essential

Transparency in the Black Box Era

Your communication style needs to be as Predictable as your services. When IT touches things, they often break. No world exists in which computer systems are perfect. In the Age of AI, this gets even more complex, as decisions become more opaque.

If you want Predictable Operations, you must build Predictable Communication.

Communication is not just a soft skill or a feel-good check-in, but rather the *connective tissue* that holds your systems, teams, and stakeholders together. Without it, your people rely on rumor, half-truths, or guesswork. Decisions get made in the dark. Commitments slip. Trust erodes.

In operations, trust and communication are one and the same. **A commitment means nothing if no one knows it's been made or changed.**

CHAPTER 5 RULE #5—COMMUNICATION IS ESSENTIAL

The truth is that Predictable Ops leaders don't just communicate when something is perfect or complete. They communicate when it's messy, when it's uncertain, and when it's bad news. This is how you prevent surprises, and surprise is the mortal enemy of predictability.

Predictable Leaders set a cadence:

- They speak before they're asked.
- They update even when there's no "final answer."
- They say *what they know, what they don't, and what they're doing to find out.*

And they teach their teams to do the same, especially now, when AI tools are making decisions that may be correct, but are not always explainable. If you can't communicate your uncertainty, you can't preserve trust. If you can't explain what just happened, you'll spend more time repairing relationships than systems.

So before you think about QBRs, maintenance windows, or outage reports, think about the bedrock: **Your ability to say, "Here's what's happening. Here's what we're doing about it. Here's what we'll do next if this plan fails."**

When your people know they'll get the truth, they'll stand by you when the unexpected does happen.

In the pages that follow, you'll see the practical side of this idea and the operational mechanics that make Predictable Communication a daily discipline, not just a leadership slogan.

Communication is a pillar of Track 1—**Operational Trust**. When you speak early, clearly, and honestly, **especially** when things go wrong, you keep trust strong even in unpredictable moments.

CHAPTER 5   RULE #5—COMMUNICATION IS ESSENTIAL

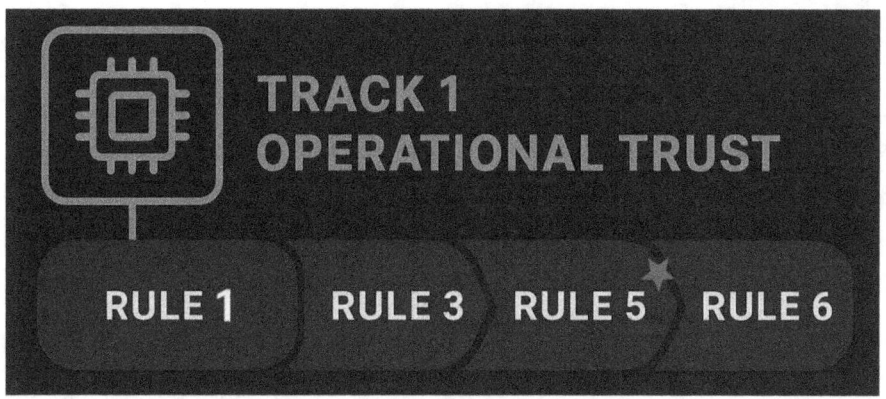

Chapter Topics—Rule #5—Communication Is Essential

- Know Your Audience
- Set the Cadence: Deadlines and Business Reviews
- Planned Disruptions: Maintenance Schedules
- Unplanned Disruptions: Speak First, Fix Fast
- Communicating Technology Changes
- IT Policies and Governance
- AI: Amplifier and Risk Multiplier
- Take a Risk and Prompt the AI
- Chapter Summary

Know Your Audience

Predictable communication starts with one immutable truth: **No two audiences hear the same message the same way.**

CHAPTER 5   RULE #5—COMMUNICATION IS ESSENTIAL

As an Ops leader, you do more than just broadcast updates. You must translate them for the people who depend on you. The right message for your front-line support team may not be the right message for your exec sponsors, your business partners, or your end customers.

Before you send a status update, a roadmap change, or an outage alert, ask yourself two questions:

Who needs to know?
What do they actually care about?
In other words, understand the function behind the face.

For example, your video conferencing team probably cares about latency, call routing, and user experience continuity. They don't need a deep dive on billing or compliance, but your finance partners absolutely do. The same maintenance window might mean a revenue impact for Sales and an SLA risk for Customer Success, so you'd better speak to both.

When you don't tailor your message, you create confusion or (worse) a silence that others will fill for you. Predictable Leaders get this right by mapping stakeholders *before* they speak. That way, the update hits home and trust stays intact.

It's not enough to be transparent. You must be *relevant*. Know who cares about what before you open your mouth.

This table may also be referenced in the Appendix as Table C-4.

CHAPTER 5   RULE #5—COMMUNICATION IS ESSENTIAL

Table 5-1. *Audience Tiers Comms Matrix*

Audience Tier	What They Care About	How You Should Communicate
Executives and Sponsors	Risk, cost impact, customer trust, high-level status, big milestones	Keep it short and strategic. Highlight business impact, major risks, and actions. No deep technical noise.
Frontline Teams	Day-to-day impact, workarounds, clear tasks, who's responsible for what	Be detailed and practical. Use clear timelines, contacts, and next steps.
Partners and Vendors	Integration points, SLAs, shared responsibilities, contract obligations	Be explicit about dependencies. Show how it affects their commitments and timelines.
Customers and End Users	Direct service impact, downtime, fixes, when normal will return	Keep it simple and human. Avoid jargon. Set expectations honestly and update when things change.

Set the Cadence: Deadlines and Business Reviews

Knowing your audience means you understand what they care about, but understanding isn't enough. You have to deliver updates and commitments in a rhythm they can trust. Predictable communication is built on a steady cadence: the promises you make, the status you share, and the reviews that keep everyone aligned. Without it, even the best audience awareness is just theory.

107

CHAPTER 5   RULE #5—COMMUNICATION IS ESSENTIAL

Committing to Deadlines

I have a standing rule for my team that sounds like common sense but is harder to implement than most people realize:

> **"If you commit to a delivery date, meet that date. If you realize you can't, tell me and the customer before the deadline passes."**

Let's break this into its two essential parts.

Meet the Date

When your team commits to a delivery date, it must not be treated as arbitrary. Your customers build their own timelines and dependencies around your commitment. A Predictable team understands this and delivers accordingly.

A team that consistently meets its deadlines earns trust and is viewed as decisive (see Rule #8) and reliable (see Rule #6). Meeting deadlines is about **thoughtful, realistic commitments**. That requires discipline, not bravado.

Leaders must train their teams to ask a basic but essential question before committing:

"*Can I realistically meet that date?*"

It's surprising how unnatural this introspection can be. Many people overcommit because they want to please:

- "Sure, I can have that by tomorrow."
- "End of the week? No problem!"
- "We'll get that done before then!"

Once these off-the-cuff comments are interpreted as commitments, things change.

Compare the above with

- "Let me see if it's possible to get that done by tomorrow."
- "Happy to help. Just let me check what else I've committed to."
- "That'll need to go through [so-and-so]; I'll follow up and get back to you."

These aren't evasions. They're examples of **honest intent backed by analysis.** You aren't saying no. You're saying, "I take your request seriously, and I'll treat it with the respect it deserves."

This small shift creates big value. Customers begin to say

"I can trust that team. When they give a date, they've thought it through. They understand the work. They know what they're doing."

Inform Before You Miss

Nobody meets every deadline. That's reality. And most professionals know well in advance when they're going to miss one. Instead of owning up to it, many wait until the last minute to surface the issue or merely stay miserably silent.

Being Predictable doesn't mean hitting every deadline. It means your partners and customers know two things:

1. You're willing to make real commitments.
2. You'll notify them early if something changes.

Remember: A missed update *is* a missed deadline because silence is its own answer.

CHAPTER 5   RULE #5—COMMUNICATION IS ESSENTIAL

This isn't just good etiquette but good **leadership**. Blind-siding your stakeholders is unforgivable. You might think you're avoiding confrontation, but you're actually causing damage that's harder to repair than the original slip.

Imagine this:

> Your team promised to deliver a key tool to the sales org on Monday.
>
> They plan a customer presentation around it for Wednesday.
>
> You miss the Monday deadline and say nothing.
>
> They find out Tuesday night.

Now you've failed and you've embarrassed someone. That's a missed delivery and a broken partnership.

Most people are reasonable. They'll be disappointed, maybe even frustrated, but if you *warn them in advance*, you earn something more valuable than praise: **their respect.**

·AI· PROMPT THE AI—FORECAST THE RISK OF MISSING A COMMITMENT

AI can help you keep your commitments honest. By ingesting historical data on similar requests like team workload, delivery performance, issue complexity, etc., you can prompt AI to **flag likely deadline misses before they happen**.

Use it to validate gut instincts with data. Ask

"Based on past projects of this type, what is the likelihood we'll deliver on time?"

This doesn't replace human judgment but can strengthen it. It may even help your team develop the foresight that trust depends on.

CHAPTER 5   RULE #5—COMMUNICATION IS ESSENTIAL

TAKE A RISK—SAY "NOT YET"

Sometimes the riskiest thing you can say is "yes" when you're not sure you can deliver. The real risk—the bold move—is to pause, assess, and say, "Not yet."

This short-term discomfort builds long-term credibility. Your partners will remember you as the one who took delivery seriously enough not to guess.

Reviews with the Business

An important aspect of communication is how you present the state of your team and performance to the business. A regular cadence of Monthly Business Reviews (MBRs) or Quarterly Business Reviews (QBRs) builds trust and empowers collaborative decision-making (see Rule #6).

These reviews shouldn't be status monologues. They're a forum to align expectations, surface risks early, and strengthen the business partnership. To do this well, a Predictable Leader keeps three key points in mind.

Audience

Identify the right stakeholders for the conversation. Nobody wants to be a "tourist" in a meeting where the subject matter is meaningless to them. For example, your Finance partners may want to see budget variances and vendor spend signals but not deep dives into server patch cycles. Match the content to their domain.

Information

Simply regurgitating raw data is the same as reading from a slide deck. Droning on by reading pre-printed copy doesn't add value. You must present real insights: What's trending? What's driving it? What does it mean for them? Show them where they should focus next. This is how you move from a passive update to an engaged dialogue. Give them *Information*, not simple data.

Actionable

Always connect the information back to decisions they can make. Data that's interesting but untied to actions is just noise. The goal is to empower the business to partner with you.. For example: "This service is trending over SLA; here are two investment options to bring it back in line.

A Predictable Leader reports and helps the business decide.

> Use AI to turn raw Ops data into clear, actionable slides or talking points for your MBRs and QBRs.
>
> Example prompts:
>
> - "Summarize our last quarter's incident metrics. Highlight trends that would concern the Finance team."
> - "Given this vendor spend report, what risks or opportunities should I flag for my business stakeholders?"
> - "Draft three slide bullets that explain this KPI dip in plain language and suggest next steps we can take together."

- "Analyze this performance dataset and recommend which insights are truly actionable for the business audience."

Remember: AI can help draft your message but only you decide what matters and how to deliver it with context.

Planned Disruptions—Maintenance Schedules

Cadence works best when things go as planned, but Ops leaders know that not everything stays on the rails. Maintenance windows, upgrades, and migrations are disruptions you can see coming. How you communicate them shows whether you can translate trust into partnership or catch people off guard when they're counting on you most.

System maintenance can create real anxiety for IT teams, partners, and customers alike. Anytime you perform maintenance, whether **Changes, Adds, or Removes**, proactive communication is non-negotiable.

> **Predictable Leaders don't just fix systems; they fix the *conversation* about when, how, and who will be impacted.**

Key steps:

- **Identify the risk.** No impact vs. some disruption vs. full downtime—be honest and explicit.
- **Identify who's affected.** Spell out every team or partner who needs to plan around this.
- **Specify the window.** Publish clear start/end times for patch windows, upgrades, or fail-overs.

CHAPTER 5 RULE #5—COMMUNICATION IS ESSENTIAL

Real World Example: Patching the Unpatchable

"We don't have a regular patching schedule for our Windows and Linux servers."

Learning this from a principal engineer on a team I'd just taken over was disconcerting but not surprising. It's daunting for teams to establish regular maintenance windows, so they slip into reactive mode: scrambling for emergency patches when exploits hit the news.

When leadership doesn't provide structure, preventative work gets crowded out by urgent break-fixes.

The **Predictable Leader** tackles this pragmatically:

- **Maintenance must happen** for security, stability, and compliance.
- **Ignoring it guarantees unpredictable events** down the road.
- **Partner with the business** to make them co-owners of the plan.

How we turned it around:

- Formed a **Patching Tiger Team**: PMs, lead engineers, clear escalation path.
- Proposed **quarterly maintenance windows:**
  - *Non-production*: First month of the quarter
  - *Production*: Second month of the quarter
  - *Third month*: Emergencies only otherwise, stability holds.

CHAPTER 5   RULE #5—COMMUNICATION IS ESSENTIAL

- Mapped out Non-Prod/Prod systems and service owners.

- **Empowered the business**: We did the pre-work, then gave service owners the *choice* of day/time inside each window. They didn't fight it and they eagerly *owned it*.

The result? Buy-in that stuck, lower conflict at go-time, and far fewer "midnight fire drills" when a zero-day hit. Maintenance was no longer a surprise because it was part of our shared Predictable Ops playbook.

Quarterly Patching Rhythm

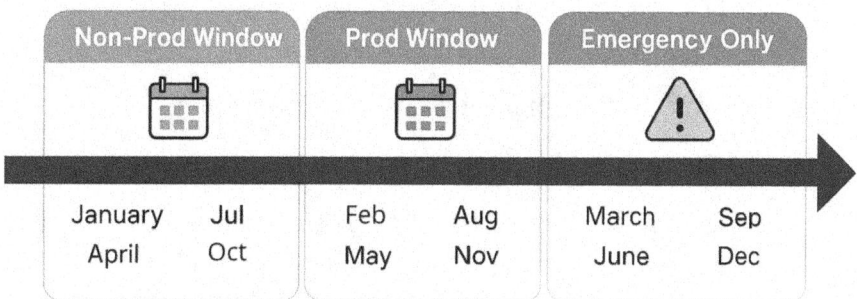

PROMPT THE AI—MAINTENANCE COUNTDOWN REMINDERS

Use AI or a simple script to automate **D-30 / D-7 / D-1** reminders for each team:

"Draft a Slack update for affected service owners: system, window, impact level, and fallback plan. Keep it under 100 words, adjust tone for executive vs. engineer."

It's a small automation, but it removes the "I didn't know" excuse forever.

115

CHAPTER 5   RULE #5—COMMUNICATION IS ESSENTIAL

Prompt the AI—Spot Service Conflicts Before You Patch

When multiple services share infrastructure, a single maintenance window can create hidden conflicts like overlapping dependencies, cascading downtime, or poor failover coverage.

Try this:

Prompt:

"Here's our proposed quarterly patching plan. For each maintenance window, analyze our CMDB (or service map) to identify any services that

- *Depend on more than one component scheduled in the same window*
- *Have SLAs that conflict with proposed downtime*
- *Lack tested failover or rollback paths*

  Flag conflicts by business impact (High/Medium/Low) and suggest an alternative sequencing if needed."

Why it works:

- Surfaces hidden interdependencies buried in your CMDB or service docs
- Prioritizes conflicts so you don't get lost in false positives
- Gives you a clear conversation starter with affected teams *before* you publish the schedule

A Predictable Leader tests for real-world collisions, so they're not apologizing on the next incident bridge.

CHAPTER 5   RULE #5—COMMUNICATION IS ESSENTIAL

Unplanned Outages: Speak First, Fix Fast

Not every disruption gives you the courtesy of a calendar invite. When something breaks without warning, your carefully planned cadence snaps under pressure. This is when Predictable Leaders prove their worth: they speak first, fix fast, and keep everyone calm enough to let Ops do its job.

When something goes wrong (and it will), your immediate priority isn't just fixing the problem. It's **communicating that you know it exists, you're on it, and you'll keep people informed until it's resolved.** Teams are under pressure to restore service faster than ever, with customers expecting real-time updates as the impact to the business grows minute-by-minute.

In Predictable Ops, silence is more damaging than the outage itself. If you let rumors, assumptions, or half-answers fill the void, you're giving people every reason to lose trust in your operations. "Speak first, fix fast" is the rhythm that keeps customers, partners, and execs calm enough to let you do your job.

Silence is worse than downtime. If you're not telling the story, someone else will and you can guarantee that you won't like *their* version. Speed and communication are now the competitive advantage. AI can transform how we detect, communicate, and resolve these incidents.

> ### ·AI· PROMPT THE AI—RAPID INCIDENT UPDATES

When something breaks, your credibility rides on how clear and consistent your updates are, just as much as how fast you fix it. The reality? On a 2 AM bridge call, good grammar and calm, consistent tone can evaporate.

That's why our incident response teams began to use AI to tighten every incident update from high-priority outages to ongoing status checks for less critical tickets. It ensures we get the technical details right *and* keep the messaging clean, consistent, and readable for every audience.

Try this:

Prompt:

"Based on this incident timeline and Slack transcript, draft a 100-word customer update in plain language. Use the T-M-P-R format (Time, Mitigation, Progress, Resolution). Flag any gaps that need confirmation before we send."

Why it works:

- Keeps updates clear under pressure with no spelling errors, no jargon overload.
- Creates a consistent tone that **execs, partners, and customers** can trust.
- Surfaces missing details or conflicting facts you may overlook in the heat of the moment.

Your job is to tell the story before someone else does. **Speak first, fix fast, and let your AI tool keep your words as steady as your plan.**

Technology Changes

Once you've earned trust during the unexpected, you have to protect it when you roll out change on purpose. Technology shifts including new platforms, decommissions, and major upgrades affect every audience differently. Getting the messaging right is what keeps your next big move from becoming your next big outage.

Unexpected changes to how technology functions are, for lack of a better term, *terrifying* to many end-users.

CHAPTER 5   RULE #5—COMMUNICATION IS ESSENTIAL

Imagine your automobile manufacturer suddenly performs a remote update to your keyless entry system. Instead of pressing the familiar button on your key fob, you're now expected to do something completely unfamiliar, and with no warning. You try unlocking your car as usual, and it doesn't work. In that moment, your confusion can quickly spiral into panic.

When you eventually discover the change was part of a "security update" no one told you about, your frustration is justified. *How dare they make a change that locks you out without any notice?*

Now take that scenario and apply it to the tools your employees use every day. When the technology they rely on suddenly changes without explanation or notice, it creates confusion, distrust, and resentment.

Even worse? When the changes involve **AI**.

It's one thing to replace a reporting tool. It's another to introduce a generative AI agent that rewrites how tasks are performed, or worse, raises fears of job loss. The emotional leap from concern to *abject horror* is real. That's why *any* technology change, not just those involving AI, must be communicated with maximum ***clarity and empathy.***

Give people time to prepare. Show them what's coming. Highlight the benefits while acknowledging the pain of transformation. If they know what to expect, they'll forgive the risks. When you surprise them, you lose their trust.

Strong communication makes the difference. And strong partnerships (see Rule #6) help you know *how* to communicate and *what* will land best with your teams and your business.

> **⌐AI⌐ PROMPT THE AI—AUDIENCE IMPACT MAP**

"Based on this planned system change, list which stakeholders are affected and what they'll want to know (impact, timeline, risk, mitigation). Flag any groups that might have unique concerns."

IT Policies and Governance

As we discussed in creating a culture of documentation, policies are a critical area of documentation. However, all too frequently even when IT leaders create policies or document them, they make several important mistakes in the process. These include

- **Created in A Vacuum** – Failure to partner with all the key stakeholders such as Legal, HR, and engineering teams.

- **Minimal-to-No Communication** – The policies get created but are severely under communicated, which creates an awareness gap across the business.

- **Lack of Enforcement** – Policies get created but have no teeth to them, resulting in zero net effect from the policy.

- **Missing Policies for Compliance** – Often caused by lack of awareness and partnership, IT teams will fail to have the appropriate policies that cover audit and compliance requirements. This can be a massive risk to the overall business.

- **Weak Governance and Oversight** – Policies often become stale over time due to a lack of regular review. As the business evolves and laws change, a lack of rigor around oversight by IT and their partners in the business makes policies no longer relevant.

The Predictable Leader makes policy development and governance a central part of their operations. It makes navigating within the IT environment **Predictable** for your team, your partners, your business, and your auditors.

Many common frameworks such as NIST, ISO-#####, TISAX, and others have comprehensive lists of required IT policies. Predictable Ops policies often follow these and can make your journey in developing your own framework much more streamlined.

Common IT Policy and Compliance Frameworks

Framework/ Standard	Focus Area	Example Policy Requirements
NIST Cybersecurity Framework (CSF)	Cybersecurity best practices	Access Control Policy, Incident Response Plan, Asset Management Policy
NIST SP 800-53	Security and Privacy controls for federal systems	Configuration Management, Security Assessment, Media Protection
ISO/IEC 27001	Information Security Management System (ISMS)	Information Security Policy, Risk Assessment Policy, Supplier Security Policy

(*continued*)

CHAPTER 5   RULE #5—COMMUNICATION IS ESSENTIAL

Framework/ Standard	Focus Area	Example Policy Requirements
ISO/IEC 27701	Privacy Information Management	Data Protection Policy, Data Retention Policy, Privacy Impact Assessment
SOC 2 (Trust Services Criteria)	Security, Availability, Confidentiality, Processing Integrity, Privacy	Change Management Policy, Logical Access Policy, Vendor Management Policy
TISAX	Automotive industry information security	Classification Guidelines, Secure Development, Third-Party Access Policies
PCI DSS	Payment card industry security	Acceptable Use Policy, Data Encryption Policy, Vulnerability Management Policy
HIPAA	US healthcare data protection	Privacy Policy, Security Rule Implementation Policies, Breach Notification Policy
GDPR	EU personal data protection	Privacy Policy, Data Subject Rights Policy, Data Processing Agreement Policies

⌞AI⌝ AI Transformation: A New Kind of Change

No major technology shift today happens without AI lurking somewhere in the mix. AI can help you spot issues, draft updates, and summarize status in ways you couldn't do alone, but it can also create noise and confusion

CHAPTER 5 RULE #5—COMMUNICATION IS ESSENTIAL

if you don't communicate what the machine can't explain. That's why you need to treat AI as both an amplifier and a risk multiplier for your message.

The Age of AI is introducing an altogether different sort of technology transformation. It's a change in *decision making*, often happening at machine speeds.

This is fundamentally different from past transformations. When email replaced paper memos, when Zoom replaced conference rooms, or when cloud platforms replaced server closets, the tools changed but the decisions were still made by people. AI flips that. The tools are now making decisions on our behalf.

That's what makes this transformation so unsettling for many. It's not just the *how* that changes, it's the *who*. Who decides what gets prioritized? Who interprets the data? Who flags the risk? In AI-assisted systems, these answers shift toward the machine.

Even when AI is working well, this can create anxiety. When it fails, the consequences are amplified.

That's why transparency is essential. Your stakeholders need to know what the AI is doing, how it's being guided, and when a human will step in. When done poorly, AI transformation feels like losing control. When done well, it feels like gaining a partner. The difference is communication.

AI, automation, and complex algorithms increasingly make decisions that affect operations, customers, compliance, and risk exposure. Even experts can't always explain why a model makes a particular decision. This can erode trust, drive resistance to adoption, and create regulatory risks.

Old Tech Change vs. AI Transformation

Feature	Old Tech Change	AI Transformation
What changes	Tools	Tools + Decision Logic
Who adapts	Human	Human + Machine

(continued)

CHAPTER 5   RULE #5—COMMUNICATION IS ESSENTIAL

Feature	Old Tech Change	AI Transformation
Trust risk	Moderate	High
Speed of impact	Gradual	Instantaneous

The table above is intended to help drive **how** you frame communication for AI transformation. Your customers, your team, and your business must be aware that as AI is introduced into your environment, whether it is via Generative AI, AI Ops, Adaptive AI, RAG integrations, and so forth, the WHAT, the WHO, the RISK, and the IMPACT are all going to transform as well.

The Predictable Leader launches AI tools and *explains them* as they progress. They prepare their teams for the shift, highlight what's changing (and what's not), and build trust around the role AI will play.

Chapter Summary—Rule #5—Communication Is Essential

This Rule strengthens **Track 1—Operational Trust** by making clarity and candor your default operating mode.

A Predictable Leader knows that communication is the thread that ties every operational promise to real trust. You tailor your updates with the same truth for every audience so no one fills in the blanks for you. That starts with *knowing who needs what:* executives want risk clarity and spend impact; frontline teams want practical details; partners need to see dependencies; customers want honesty without surprises.

When it comes to commitments, cadence beats crisis. You build trust by setting clear deadlines, keeping business reviews steady, and owning the roadmap, even when the path shifts. Planned disruptions like maintenance windows and upgrades don't have to erode confidence when you handle them with early, specific messaging that turns downtime into partnership, not panic.

But not every outage gives you a courtesy heads-up. When things break unexpectedly, "speak first, fix fast" is your mantra. Silence is more damaging than the failure itself. When you don't tell the story, people will write one for you. The same goes for technology changes: the bigger the shift, the clearer you must be about what's changing, who's affected, and how you'll guide them through it.

Finally, AI has changed the game but only if you use it wisely. Tools like CoPilot and ChatGPT can tighten your updates, flag missing details, and reduce the gap between raw data and clear status. But they can't explain uncertainty or take responsibility for what happens next. That's your job.

Remember: Solid communication builds trust and confidence. Outcomes are more transparent when decisions are explained.

Predictable Leaders don't hide behind the machine. They speak early, adjust often, and keep trust stronger than any outage or roadmap surprise.

CHAPTER 6

Rule #6—Be a Trusted Partner

Collaborating with AI and Everyone Else

A Predictable Leader seeks out challenges and actively partners with colleagues to solve them. As AI becomes an essential part of how we plan, operate, and deliver, the most Predictable force in your organization must still be you. Trust is more than just being there when things break. Trust is built by proving you can construct what comes next. Delivering day-to-day builds credibility. Delivering the big bets cements trust that you can help the business grow. You need to do more than just keep the lights on.

You can't lead effectively if people don't trust you.

That may sound obvious, but in IT (and especially in IT operations) trust isn't built the way most people think.

Many leaders assume that delivering reliable results is enough. If the servers stay up, the systems are patched, and the KPIs are green, then trust should naturally follow. But trust in leadership, especially in a world increasingly shaped by AI-driven decisions, requires something more than performance. It requires presence. It requires partnership.

CHAPTER 6 RULE #6—BE A TRUSTED PARTNER

To be a Predictable Leader, you must be more than just a technical expert. You must be seen as a collaborator: someone who listens, communicates clearly, owns their decisions, and engages proactively with others across the business. You must be someone who can be counted on in the moment, over time, and when it really matters.

This is especially true in the Age of AI, where trust is more than just about outcomes. Trust includes understanding the systems that generate those outcomes. When machines start making recommendations or decisions, your peers and stakeholders will look to you. Not just for answers, but for confidence. Should we trust this insight? Should we automate this process? Should we act on this recommendation?

They won't be asking the AI for permission.

They'll be asking YOU.

That trust doesn't arrive with your title. It is earned through relationship, transparency, accountability, and time.

Partnership is built on Track 1—**Operational Trust**. When people see that you deliver, show up early, partner with sincerity, and keep them informed, they know they can count on you when stakes are high.

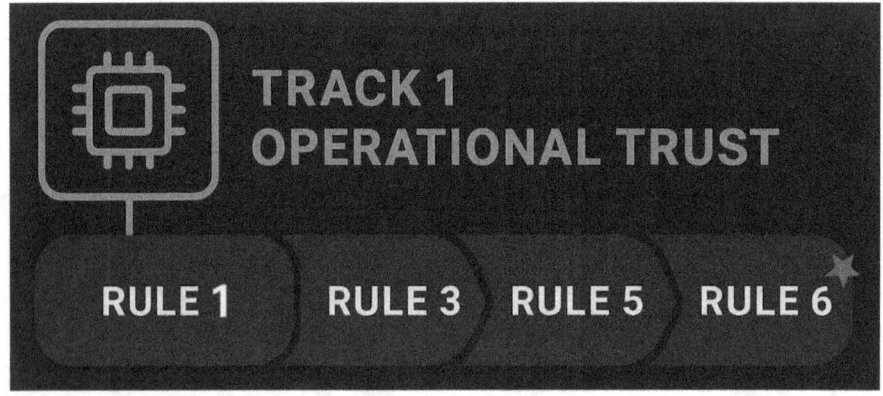

CHAPTER 6 RULE #6—BE A TRUSTED PARTNER

Chapter Topics—Rule #6—Be a Trusted Partner

- Predictability Builds Confidence
- Beyond Performance—The Human Connection
- Building Personal Trust
- Build Relationships
- Trust Is a Prerequisite to Transformation
- Aligning on Priorities
- Delivering Major Initiatives
- The AI Pitch
- Take a Risk and Prompt the AI
- Chapter Summary

Predictability Builds Confidence, Confidence Enables Evolution

Trust isn't declared. It's built slowly, methodically, and behaviorally. It can be reinforced every time you do what you say you'll do.

The foundation of Predictable Ops is built on trust-generating behaviors:

- **You deliver when you say you will.**

    (Rule #3—Develop Your Team: Drive Accountability)

- **You communicate proactively about risks.**

    (Rule #5—Communication Is Essential: Communicate Honestly)

- **You document how things work and what will change.**

    (Rule #1—Operations Should Be Boring: Build a Culture of Documentation)

- **You admit when you're wrong and fix what breaks.**

    (Predictable Ops: Lead Transparently, Iterate Honestly)

- **You show consistency across weeks, months, and quarters.**

    (Rule #2—Measure What Matters: Review with Discipline)

These aren't technical practices, they're leadership habits. They form a pattern your business partners begin to notice. And over time, they form a story your organization starts to believe: *"This team shows up. This team follows through."*

> Before your peers will trust AI-assisted decision-making, they need to trust your decision-making.
>
> Before they buy into automation, they need to believe your team won't disappear the moment something goes sideways.
>
> Predictable Ops earns that belief—because it demonstrates, consistently, that your systems, your team, and your leadership can be counted on.

When that belief is in place, your next conversation about transformation (such as introducing AI) doesn't feel like a gamble. It feels like evolution.

CHAPTER 6   RULE #6—BE A TRUSTED PARTNER

Beyond Performance—The Human Connection

Predictable Ops is more than uptime, incident response, or managing budgets. Relationships with real people are critical to operational success. People don't form trust with metrics. They form trust with humans.

You can't automate trust. You earn it through intentional connection.

Being proactive in this area means reaching out *even when there are no problems.* It means regularly checking in with your peers, listening without an agenda, and staying plugged in to their needs even when everything is "working."

You might assume that consistent performance is enough to earn trust. It isn't. Performance earns respect. But trust? That comes from shared experience, open communication, and human rapport. People trust those who show up *when they're not required to.* They seek out those who offer help without being asked, who admit when they're unsure, and who genuinely care about outcomes beyond their own department.

In the age of AI, this human connection becomes even more vital. As systems grow more autonomous, your personal leadership becomes the anchor for confidence. The more abstract and fast-moving the technology, the more your team and your peers need to know there's a steady hand behind it. More than just a high performer, but a trusted partner.

Predictability is as much about behavior as it is about systems, and how consistently, transparently, and relationally you deliver.

Because at the end of the day, trust is built on *how you treat people along the way.*

CHAPTER 6   RULE #6—BE A TRUSTED PARTNER

TAKE A RISK—THE DIFFICULT HUMAN CONNECTION

Some of the most valuable relationships in your organization are the hardest to build.

You know the type. The director who never responds. The VP who bristles at any suggestion outside their lane. The partner team that insists on doing things "their way." It's easy to label them as obstacles, and even easier to work around them entirely.

But Predictable Leaders don't avoid these challenges. They lean into them.

Approach the conversation. Offer a coffee. Share your goals and ask about theirs. You may not walk away best friends, but you've opened a door. Over time, that all becomes the foundation for a stronger partnership.

Don't underestimate the power of human connection. Sometimes, the biggest transformation doesn't come from a new tool or process. True connection can come from a handshake and a hard conversation.

Take the risk. Go first. Build the bridge.

 Real World Example—Repairing a Relationship

Early in my IT career, I got off on the worst possible foot with a senior engineer. We had similar personalities, and we constantly clashed, sometimes bitterly and even personally. At the time, the issues felt important enough to "die on that mountain," but in hindsight, I was simply being more obstinate than I needed to be.

CHAPTER 6   RULE #6—BE A TRUSTED PARTNER

A seasoned manager of mine noticed. I would vent to him after yet another disagreement, and he'd listen in quiet contemplation. Then, toward the end of the year, he surprised me with a challenge:

> "One of the goals I'm setting for you is to make that engineer your ally. I'll be judging your performance based on how well you build that bridge."

I was stunned. How could I possibly repair a relationship that seemed doomed from the start?

What I didn't realize was that the senior engineer *also* wanted to improve the relationship. I wouldn't have known had I not been vulnerable and willing to make the human connection.

To my surprise, it didn't take long but it did take effort. I invited him to lunch. I made sure to chat with him in the hallway. We aligned our meeting attendance. Slowly, the tension gave way to mutual understanding. We realized we shared the same goals, and within six months, we became strong partners delivering real business outcomes.

The lesson was clear: **unpredictable relationships can become Predictable** through honest effort and an eagerness to partner without ego.

Building Personal Trust—Show Up, Speak Honestly, Ask for Help

Operational excellence doesn't exist in a vacuum. To be a trusted partner, people must see you not just as capable but as approachable. One of the most powerful tools you have is vulnerability.

Trust deepens when leaders are willing to ask for help. Whether it's convening an IT Steering Committee to review tooling, operations, or roadmap planning, or simply checking in with a peer to say, "I don't have this figured out yet". These moments of transparency matter. They show your colleagues that partnership isn't a slogan. It's how you lead.

You'll still need to perform, communicate clearly, and deliver consistently. But if you want to be trusted when things go sideways (and they will), you need to build relational credit long before that happens.

We ask for help constantly in life, without shame, without hesitation. Can you pass the salt? Hold the door? Lend a hand? But something shifts in a work setting. We start to believe that asking for help is a sign of weakness, or worse, that it gives someone power over us.

Nothing could be further from the truth.

When you ask a peer or partner for help, you're not diminishing your value, rather you're inviting them to share in the outcome. Most people *want* to be helpful. It validates their expertise and builds mutual confidence. In fact, few things build trust faster than being asked to contribute to something meaningful.

You should feel as comfortable asking a partner for help as you would asking someone to pass you a napkin at dinner.

Humility is what makes you relatable. It turns leaders into collaborators and performance into partnership.

Build Relationships

You are not allowed to lead in a vacuum.

The leader who isolates themselves, who only communicates through reports, metrics, and incident updates, will eventually be seen as replaceable. Worse, they may be actively excluded from critical discussions that shape the future of the business. Predictable leadership requires more than operational consistency. It requires human connection.

Relationships are your force multiplier. When your partners know who you are, when they've seen you show up in moments of stress and ambiguity, when you've listened to their frustrations and helped them succeed, they will turn to you again. They will trust you to help them make difficult decisions. They will back your proposals. They will invite you into conversations that others only hear about later.

This isn't political. It's professional.

In today's environment, building relationships is strategic. Especially in the era of AI, where decisions will increasingly be influenced by systems and data pipelines, not just people. If you're not known as someone who can explain, contextualize, and lead through this shift, then someone else will fill that role.

Building strong relationships begins with a few simple but powerful practices:

- **Be Present** – Don't hide behind your inbox. Show up to meetings, one-on-ones, and project kickoffs. Be visible, and be someone people feel they can approach.

- **Be Curious** – Ask questions. Seek to understand the goals and frustrations of your business partners before offering solutions. Listen more than you speak.

- **Be Useful** – Look for ways to be helpful, even when it's not in your immediate scope. Share context, connect dots, make introductions. Be seen as a trusted ally, not just a service provider.

- **Be Consistent** – Trust is built over time, not during a single crisis. Show that you're someone who follows through especially when no one's watching.

This matters even more when AI becomes part of the operational picture.

AI in IT is a team sport: engineers, data scientists, platform teams, product managers, and business stakeholders all play a role. Predictable Ops leaders who invest in those relationships now will be best positioned to lead AI transformation later. When it comes time to explain *why the algorithm suggested that change*, or *how the AI flagged that early warning signal*, your credibility will hinge on the trust you've built even more than just the accuracy of the output.

CHAPTER 6   RULE #6—BE A TRUSTED PARTNER

The AI age will reward the leader who is not only technically fluent but relationally fluent. Build those bridges now, and you'll be ready to lead across them.

⦁AI⦁ PROMPT THE AI—ANALYZE YOUR RELATIONSHIP PATTERNS

Predictable Leaders don't just build systems—they build trust. But over time, even the best leaders can fall into patterns: meeting with the same people, defaulting to familiar alliances, or avoiding more difficult personalities.

Upload your 1:1 meeting data from the past 6–12 months: calendar exports, meeting titles, attendees. Include upcoming schedules if possible. Then prompt the AI.

- "Analyze which individuals I meet with most frequently. Who are my top ten collaborators by meeting count?"
- "Identify any key stakeholders in [org/team list] that I haven't met with in the past three months."
- "Are there leaders I'm over-indexing on? Under-engaging?"
- "Based on these patterns, what risks do you see to cross-functional alignment?"
- "Suggest a more balanced engagement schedule based on role, influence, and project overlap."

The goal is to illuminate your relationships. The right prompt can reveal who's in your circle…and who's missing from it.

☐ *Tool Tip: If you're in a Microsoft 365 environment, ask CoPilot to analyze your 1:1 meeting patterns. Use it as a lens on where you're leaning in and where you may be leaning away.*

CHAPTER 6   RULE #6—BE A TRUSTED PARTNER

Trust Is a Prerequisite to Transformation

No team or business unit will embrace AI tools from IT if they don't trust IT to begin with.

Predictable Operations are a statement of efficiency and reliability. When services run smoothly, issues are resolved quickly, and communication is clear and consistent, your business partners begin to rely on you for insight and leadership. That's the trust you must earn before introducing AI into the equation.

AI introduces a new layer of abstraction, uncertainty, and (for many) unease. If your partners don't trust the underlying operations involving the humans, the processes, and the discipline, then they certainly won't trust automation, generative outputs, or machine-led decision support.

Trust is the bedrock of transformation. And in IT, trust is always earned behaviorally.

AI is a shift in how decisions are made, how work gets done, and how people interpret outcomes. When a machine generates a recommendation that affects budget, staffing, or customer experience, your business partners will ask: "Where did this come from? Why should I trust it?"

If your team is known for transparency, stability, and partnership, they'll trust your answer. If you're seen as reactive, disconnected, or inconsistent, they'll push back, or worse, disengage entirely.

Predictable Ops lays the groundwork for AI adoption by demonstrating what responsible leadership looks like. It says

- "We already operate with discipline and foresight."
- "We already communicate proactively and honestly."
- "We already deliver results our business partners can count on."

When AI is layered on top of that operational maturity, it's powerful. It becomes an extension of the trust you've already built, not a threat to it.

So before you ask your organization to take the leap into AI, prove that you're already leading with the kind of clarity, consistency, and transparency that makes transformation possible.

Aligning on Priorities

We've now taken the journey through Track 1 to build operational trust. So the next logical question is: *Have you done all you need to do to be a trusted partner?*

The answer is *not quite*. Personal trust is just the beginning. You must also ensure that your **priorities** align with those of your business partners. In an ideal world, everyone is working toward the same outcomes that are clear, aligned, and consistent across the organization.

Sadly, that's rarely the case.

In reality, priorities and goals can diverge sharply from leader to leader. That's why so much of your energy in partnership conversations must be spent on **aligning direction**. Not assuming it. *Confirming it.* You have to calibrate together, again and again.

If trusted relationships don't translate into shared priorities, then Predictability collapses. You may have the relationship, but you're pulling in different directions. And when that happens?

You fail.

To maintain alignment, trusted partners embed themselves in each other's rhythms. Here are some proven ways to stay aligned:

- **Occasionally attend each other's staff meetings.** This keeps both sides grounded in operational reality, not just strategy.

- **Cocreate presentations for brown bag sessions, all-hands meetings, and exec briefings.** It ensures the message is shared. Shared ownership builds trust.

- **Join the same business strategy meetings.** (See Rule #7—Plug into the Future of Your Business.) If you're not in the room, you're not in the plan.

- **Collaboratively review each other's contract renewals.** To maintain alignment, and to surface risks, constraints, and opportunities before the pressure hits.

- **Sync on quarterly goals.** Deep-dive updates, with a true look at how each team's deliverables enable the other's success.

- **Run a joint retrospective.** Look back at a project or quarter together. What worked? What didn't? What surprised you?

- **Share roadmaps early.** Don't wait for a launch or exec review. Proactively show each other what's coming so you can align ahead of time.

- **Keep a running alignment doc.** It doesn't have to be formal. Even a shared bullet list of evolving priorities, open risks, and assumptions can avoid misfires.

- **Invite feedback on your own operations.** Ask how your team's performance is affecting theirs, and mean it.

- **Offer to represent them when they're not in the room.** Ask them to do the same. Trusted partners speak each other's names with confidence.

CHAPTER 6   RULE #6—BE A TRUSTED PARTNER

TAKE A RISK—INVITE A SENIOR LEADER

As mentioned above, occasionally attending other teams' staff meetings is a great way to maintain trust and alignment. But here's another technique worth trying: *invite a senior leader to speak at a meeting you're hosting.*

At first glance, this might seem like "kissing up," but if you've already established some rapport through relationship building, the risk of that perception is minimal. In fact, many senior leaders welcome the opportunity to share their perspective, reinforce strategic goals, and connect directly with the broader team.

Meetings they're most likely to say yes to and make an impact in include

- Staff Meetings
- Team Strategy Sessions
- Project Review Meetings
- Budget Planning or Review Sessions
- Department All-Hands

Think about a senior leader who could inspire your team or help reinforce alignment across functions. Take the risk. Extend the invite. The worst they can say is no, and the best outcome is a renewed sense of clarity, trust, and shared direction.

> **⊡ PROMPT THE AI—SEE WHO'S MISSING FROM THE CONVERSATION**

AI can help you step back and see your network of leadership engagement more clearly. Upload your 1:1 meeting logs, stakeholder maps, or team calendar events into an AI tool and ask it to identify

- Which senior leaders you've met with recently and how often
- Who hasn't been engaged in the past 3–6 months
- Which meetings could benefit from leadership presence based on org impact or timing
- Suggested talking points based on current org initiatives

For example, prompt

> "Based on this meeting history, which senior leaders have I not connected with in the past quarter? What upcoming meetings could be a good opportunity to bring them in?"

Tools like Microsoft CoPilot and Google Duet already integrate this logic into email, calendar, and document activity. Use it to find the gaps, so you can fill them with real conversations that build Predictable trust.

Delivering Major Initiatives: The Ultimate Trust Builder

Availability, partnership, and trust are built one day at a time. They're cemented when you deliver the big promises. Major transformations are the ultimate trust tests. When you show you can run the business and change it at the same time, you're a partner in its future.

CHAPTER 6   RULE #6—BE A TRUSTED PARTNER

Being a trusted partner is oftentimes about showing up for the big moments. The ones that test your credibility, your technical depth, and your leadership all at once.

Real World Example: Partnering for Major Transformation

When I led the operations team for our email archiving service, we faced one of those moments: moving the entire platform from physical datacenters to the cloud.

That meant **hundreds of billions of small files**, *petabytes* of storage, and **hundreds of terabytes of database files**—all shifting from on-premises racks we'd managed for years to a distributed, cloud-native backbone.

Success was never guaranteed.

The risks were real: data integrity, performance, security, cost overruns, migration downtime. Because this service touched nearly every part of the company, success demanded more than good infrastructure planning. Success required trust, constant communication, and shared ownership across **DevOps, Software Engineering, Cloud Vendors, Executive Leadership, and Customer Success.**

Trust was built daily.

I didn't just set the plan and disappear. I stayed *visibly connected* to the delivery team, showing up in stand-ups, removing blockers, and surfacing issues early to execs so they never got blindsided. I made sure our partners, especially the engineering and customer success teams, understood the migration phases and could explain them to customers with confidence. And when the plan had to change (because it always does), I owned the story. That meant sharing what we knew, what we didn't yet know, and exactly how we were testing our assumptions.

CHAPTER 6   RULE #6—BE A TRUSTED PARTNER

Credibility came from being real about risk.

I never pretended there wouldn't be bumps. I called out tough trade-offs early, asked the team to stress-test our fallback plans, and made sure no one hid bad news. When we hit our milestones and maintained customer SLAs without major surprises, the result wasn't just a technical win. It was a trust dividend. People knew we could run the business and change it at the same time.

When the stakes are high, Predictable Leaders don't vanish behind the Gantt chart. They stay present, name the risks out loud, and prove they'll be there to fix what breaks. That's the foundation of trust.

TAKE A RISK—PUT YOUR NAME ON THE BIG MOVE

You don't build trust on a project like this by hiding behind process. Put your name on it. Own the plan, the risks, the decision points, the communications. When people know you'll stand by the outcome, they'll lean in to make it succeed because you've shown you're not running when it gets hard.

 ## The AI Pitch

At some point, perhaps sooner than you think, you'll be collaborating not just with human partners, but with AI. This isn't science fiction. If it hasn't started for you already, it will. How smoothly you bridge the gap between human and machine partners depends on the trust you've built with people.

There will come a time when your customers, your business, and your leadership expect AI tooling to be part of everyday operations. Not as an experiment or a side project but as a core, trusted part of Predictable Ops. AI will become as ubiquitous as mobile apps, and as essential as Wi-Fi.

143

CHAPTER 6   RULE #6—BE A TRUSTED PARTNER

What you're witnessing now is the starting gun. As an IT leader, you are not on the sidelines. You are the one who shapes how quickly your team, your partners, and your organization embrace what's coming.

A word of caution: Don't expect people to trust the technology just because you do.

This is where your leadership matters most. AI is a new way of working. It changes how decisions are made, how data is interpreted, and how outcomes are delivered. That kind of change will make people uncomfortable.

Some people think of AI in Operations and imagine machine-speed automation. However, you're introducing much more than that. You're introducing algorithms that analyze customer trends, optimize system performance, and suggest actions sometimes faster than any human can keep up with. This can feel threatening to some, disorienting to others, and thrilling to a few. You need to be ready for all of it.

The pitch is less about AI's brilliance and more about your team's readiness to wield it responsibly.

- Can your operations handle the speed of machine insights?
- Can your partners rely on the transparency of your AI-enabled decisions?
- Can you explain how an AI model is being trained, evaluated, and applied?
- And most importantly: can you be trusted to know when to **override the machine**?

These are the questions that will define how fast your organization moves forward or how long it hesitates.

Predictable Ops is the foundation. AI is the evolution.

CHAPTER 6   RULE #6—BE A TRUSTED PARTNER

When your partners already see you as reliable, consistent, and transparent, they're far more likely to walk with you into the next chapter. They'll follow because you've earned the right to lead.

So yes—this is a pitch. But you're not selling technology. You're selling trust. And that's the only way transformation happens.

TAKE A RISK—MAKE THE AI PITCH PERSONAL

No major transformation gets done by staying in the shadows. Put your name on it. Own the plan, the risks, the decision points, and the communication, even when the plan changes.

Quick Lessons:

Stay visible. Be in the stand-ups, the steering meetings, the hallway check-ins. If people never see you, they won't believe you're backing them when it gets hard.

Name the risk out loud. Surprises break trust; early honesty builds it. Call out trade-offs and fallback plans before they're needed.

Own the narrative. When things shift (and they will), explain what you know, what you don't, and what you'll do next. Control the story so no one has to guess.

Bottom line: *When your name is on the big move, people know you'll stand by the outcome and they'll stand by you to get it done.*

CHAPTER 6   RULE #6—BE A TRUSTED PARTNER

Leading the AI Journey

Many organizations still look to IT as the hub for making informed technology decisions. Once you've earned that trust by demonstrating real operational stability and measurable AI success within your own team, then you are uniquely positioned to guide the broader organization forward.

This isn't about owning every AI decision. It's about being a trusted partner in helping your business embrace the AI era with clarity and confidence. A Predictable Leader doesn't just lead projects, they lead transformation.

Start with measurable wins in your own team. Once trust is established, lead the way in scaling AI responsibly, aligning technology with business goals, fostering collaboration, and empowering every team to innovate.

Nearly every business unit can benefit from AI assistance. The key is helping your peers understand what's possible without overpromising, and without losing sight of the outcomes that matter. Below are just a few examples of where AI can make a meaningful difference across departments:

- **Software Engineering** – Performance analytics, code optimization, test coverage gap analysis, and GitCopilot-assisted development

- **Quality Assurance/Testing** – Automated regression testing, failure pattern detection, and machine learning to predict bugs introduced by feature changes

- **Security Operations** – Threat intelligence from large-scale log ingestion, AI-driven anomaly detection, auto-remediation of vulnerabilities, and predictive phishing prevention

- **Finance and Budgeting** – Spend forecasting, anomaly detection in vendor charges, contract compliance review, and budget modeling (see Rule #4)

- **Customer Service** – Chatbot augmentation, sentiment analysis, AI-generated response suggestions, and trend spotting in complaint logs

- **Human Resources** – Resume matching, internal mobility prediction, employee sentiment tracking, and skills gap analysis (see Rule #3)

- **Legal and Compliance** – AI-supported contract analysis, policy compliance checks, and discovery review acceleration

- **Marketing and Sales** – Lead scoring, campaign optimization, AI-written content drafts, and predictive buying behavior

- **Facilities/Real Estate** – IoT-powered energy optimization, space utilization analysis, and predictive maintenance scheduling

You don't need to be the expert in every domain but you *do* need to be a proactive partner. Being a Predictable Leader means surfacing relevant use cases, managing AI risk thoughtfully, and ensuring that the right guardrails are in place as your organization moves forward.

See **Appendix A: AI, ML, and Deep Learning Tools for the Predictable Ops Journey** for a curated list of tools you can explore and apply across your organization. This list is not exhaustive and, in all likelihood, it will evolve even before this book hits your shelf. That's the pace we're operating at.

CHAPTER 6   RULE #6—BE A TRUSTED PARTNER

The Predictable Leader constantly looks to partner closely with business units, vendors, and technical teams to evaluate which tools are the right fit for which business problems. Your role is not to be the sole decision-maker, but the informed, trusted guide.

Chapter Summary—Rule #6: Be a Trusted Partner

In the world of Predictable Ops, technical performance and operational discipline are only part of the equation. The real currency of transformation is trust. This Rule strengthens **Track 1—Operational Trust** by showing that real relationships are built on predictable performance and visible commitment.

Trust doesn't appear when you deliver a new tool or hit your uptime targets. It grows from the way you show up: when you listen, when you admit what you don't know, when you build bridges with your peers and your business partners instead of standing apart on an island of technical know-how.

Strong relationships turn you from a service provider into a strategic partner. They turn your team from "IT" into *our* team. That's the reputation you need when you introduce AI into the mix.

People won't trust the machine until they trust the human who leads it.

In that context, the Predictable Partner develops and demonstrates several key partnership strengths:

- Honest about capacity
- Proactive about cross-team goals
- Transparent with data
- Trustworthy even when it's hard

CHAPTER 6   RULE #6—BE A TRUSTED PARTNER

As AI becomes woven into your operations, it will test the depth of those partnerships. People will have questions. They'll have doubts. They'll need you to explain not just *how* things work, but *why* decisions are being made at machine speed, and *what* you'll do when the machine gets it wrong.

Your Predictable leadership is the safeguard. Your commitment to clear communication, consistent delivery, and shared accountability is what gives your peers the confidence to walk with you into this next phase.

When people know they can count on you, they'll trust you to guide them through uncertainty, human or machine.

Trust is the force multiplier for every change that follows. Build it. Sustain it. And never forget: you can't automate Trust.

CHAPTER 7

Rule #7—Prepare for the Future

The Future Is Already Here! Now What?

IT is never "future proof." Your business partners, vendors, industry, even technology itself will leave you behind if you're not actively tracking the trends that shape our world. Everything from cloud platforms to infrastructure as code to the holy grail of artificial intelligence is evolving faster than most realize. Preparing for the future is about making brave, practical moves that position your Ops for what's next while still delivering today.

How often in the past five years, or five months, or five days, or five minutes has AI been mentioned in a press release, a tech article, an executive briefing, a blog posting, or a product launch? In the mid-2020s, AI dominates the conversation, and that level of hype is not unusual in our industry.

Over the last few decades, we've seen plenty of transformative trends that reshaped the language of technology. We've referenced a few already, but the list is practically endless:

- Cloud Infrastructure
- Infrastructure as Code

CHAPTER 7   RULE #7—PREPARE FOR THE FUTURE

- Software as a Service (SaaS)
- Hyper-Converged Infrastructure
- Virtualized Infrastructure
- Zero-Trust Security
- Virtual Collaboration Tools
- Artificial Intelligence

As these trends gained traction, businesses, vendors, and entire industries shifted their strategies. Some changes were sudden. Others evolved slowly. Many are still underway. But one thing is certain: if you want to be Predictable in your space, you must stay aware. Falling behind isn't an option.

One of the biggest mistakes I've seen leaders make is trusting anyone who says, *"This will future-proof your environment."* Take those words as what they are: marketing copy. Odds are, that same vendor is already developing the next version that will render today's offering obsolete. And no one, not even the vendor, can truly predict where technology is headed. Beware of categorical claims about innovation. They almost always age poorly.

Furthermore, many leaders stay technically focused and don't understand the direction of their own business. Predictable leaders align both the wave of industry and the flow of their business to mold future strategy.

In the previous chapter, we discussed how the Predictable Leader acts as a guide through the AI journey. To be the best guide possible, you must prepare for the future.

This Rule is your call to stay in Track 2—**Preparation and Foresight** mode. **The future never stops moving. You can't predict everything**, but you can prepare by watching trends, stress-testing plans, and adjusting early.

CHAPTER 7   RULE #7—PREPARE FOR THE FUTURE

Chapter Topics—Rule #7—Prepare for the Future

- Remain Up-To-Date and Modern
- Plug into the Future of Your Business
- AI: Your Bridge Between Trends And Business Value
- Don't Fall for Trend Traps
- Build a Roadmap
- AI Transformation
- Take a Risk and Prompt the AI
- Chapter Summary

Remain Up-to-Date and Modern

Predictable leaders never fall behind the innovation curve. While you may not always have the budget or staffing to adopt the latest and greatest technologies, you must, at minimum, be educated and informed about where the industry is headed technologically, operationally, and strategically.

CHAPTER 7 RULE #7—PREPARE FOR THE FUTURE

A leader with stale information quickly loses credibility. Picture someone discussing the nuances of Windows 95 in a 2025 IT strategy session. It might sound like an obtuse example, but in today's fast-moving tech landscape, it's surprisingly easy to sound outdated, and faster than you think.

Peers, customers, vendors, and executives will ask you about emerging technologies. Some are just curious. Others are trying to make strategic decisions. A Predictable Leader can answer thoughtfully, offer insight, and guide the conversation because they've done the work to stay informed. That's what builds trust. When you're clearly out of touch, your credibility takes a hit that's hard to recover from.

Here are a few practical ways to stay informed:

- **Attend Technical Conferences**

    Your vendors can recommend relevant events and may be able to get you into sessions at little to no cost.

- **Participate in Executive Briefings**

    If your vendors have a local Executive Briefing Center, attend in person. If not, work with your VAR or vendor to set up a remote or on-site session.

- **Read—A Lot**

    Follow trusted tech blogs, industry news sites, vendor updates, and yes, even books like this one. Absorb constantly. Your ability to lead depends on it.

- **Join Peer Groups or Leadership Roundtables**

    Many regions have CIO/CTO forums, digital transformation councils, or industry-specific roundtables. These provide candid, real-world insight from leaders facing similar challenges. Some are vendor-sponsored, others are independent.

- **Participate in Vendor Roadmap Sessions**

  Ask your key vendors for roadmap briefings. These often reveal upcoming product changes, shifts in strategy, or AI feature rollouts long before they're public.

- **Use AI to Summarize Trends**

  Prompt tools like ChatGPT to generate summaries from Gartner reports, blog feeds, or product update pages. Ask for pros/cons, industry adoption trends, or use case comparisons.

- **Listen to Podcasts or Audiobooks**

  Many tech leaders use commutes or gym time to consume industry podcasts. Good ones cover current trends, interviews with practitioners, and behind-the-scenes vendor moves.

- **Follow Industry Analysts or Influencers**

  On LinkedIn, Mastodon, or Bluesky, follow thought leaders who specialize in your domain: cloud, AI, DevOps, cybersecurity, etc. Their commentary can provide early signals.

- **Experiment with Labs or Free Trials**

  Ask your team to evaluate new tools in sandbox environments. Many AI/ML or observability platforms offer limited trial periods, so use these to explore hands-on without committing budget.

- **Engage in Internal Reverse Mentoring**

  Junior engineers often adopt emerging tech faster. Set up regular syncs or brown-bag sessions where newer team members show what tools or techniques they're exploring.

TAKE A RISK—STAY INFORMED, FAST

You're not expected to know everything but you are expected to keep up. The pace of change in IT is unforgiving, and waiting for your company to "officially adopt" a technology before learning about it is a losing strategy.

Take the risk of exploring something *before* it's mainstream. Try that vendor's trial version. Ask a junior engineer to explain a tool they love. Watch the AI keynote from a vendor you don't even use. Prompt ChatGPT or CoPilot with "What's trending in IT Ops this quarter?" and see what sticks.

The real risk? Falling behind. Predictable leaders stay current because they seek, not because they're told.

Plug into the Future of *Your* Business

Staying ahead in IT also involves understanding where your *business* is going as it is, and ensuring your team, your tools, and your roadmap are aligned to support it. This can often be as important as keeping up with the wave of technology.

Too frequently, IT leaders focus exclusively on what's happening in the tech industry while remaining disconnected from the direction of their own organization. If you're not attuned to your company's goals, growth plans, customer shifts, or market pressures, then even the most advanced tech stack will miss the mark.

CHAPTER 7   RULE #7—PREPARE FOR THE FUTURE

To be Predictable, to truly prepare for the future, you must be deeply embedded in the business itself.

Ask yourself

- Do you attend product planning or strategy meetings?
- Are you part of conversations around new markets or service lines?
- Do you know what your sales and support teams hear from customers?
- Can you clearly articulate your company's top three goals this year?

If the answer to any of these is "no," it's time to change that.

Being "future-ready" means understanding not just where technology is headed, but how your specific business is evolving and what it will *need* from IT. Don't just keep up with the tech. Keep up with your business.

AI: Your Bridge Between Trends and Business Value

Staying current and staying connected are no longer separate disciplines. With the rise of AI, the Predictable Leader now has a new toolset to bridge the external pulse of innovation with the internal heartbeat of the business.

The AI tools and engines you use to track tech trends can help you spot business risks, explore new strategies, and surface insights that align IT efforts with company goals.

- **Generative AI** can summarize the latest thought leadership, Gartner reports, or vendor updates in minutes.

157

- **AI meeting assistants** can flag strategic themes from planning sessions, customer briefings, or internal all-hands.

- **ML-driven dashboards** can correlate operational data with business outcomes like churn risk, sales cycle delays, or fulfillment gaps.

- **Custom AI agents (Agentic AI)** can even be trained on internal documents (RAG), enabling your team to query internal goals, roadmaps, or support data in seconds.

The result? You stay current and you stay relevant. You're no longer chasing trends or sitting passively in the business's wake. You're helping to steer the ship.

Remember: AI is only as valuable as the foundation you've laid. Without good data, strong documentation, and business fluency, AI tools can become little more than buzzword generators. When used intentionally, however, AI becomes the connective tissue between what's coming and what matters.

·[AI]· PROMPT THE AI—STAY INFORMED ON TECH AND BUSINESS TRENDS

AI can help you cut through the noise and focus on what matters, whether you're tracking industry trends or planning for your company's next chapter. Use AI to summarize, correlate, and contextualize.

To track industry and tech trends:

- "Summarize the top five IT operations trends for this quarter."
- "What are the newest AI capabilities impacting infrastructure management?"

CHAPTER 7 RULE #7—PREPARE FOR THE FUTURE

- "What are analysts saying about the future of enterprise observability?"

To stay informed about your business context:

- "Based on these meeting transcripts, what are the recurring themes in executive strategy discussions?"
- "What customer issues have been trending over the last six months in our ticketing system?"
- "How do our IT incidents correlate with business-impacting events like product launches or sales cycles?"

To bridge both worlds:

- "Which technology trends might affect our business model in the next 12 months?"
- "What are common use cases for AI in [your industry], and which ones align with our current capabilities?"

AI won't replace your judgment but it *will* accelerate your awareness. Stay informed *and* stay aligned.

CHAPTER 7 RULE #7—PREPARE FOR THE FUTURE

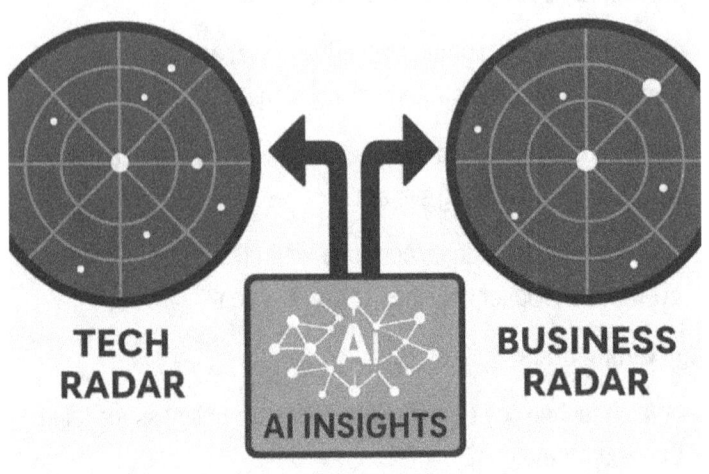

Your AI Insights will not be complete if you don't have a sharp radar for Tech and Business trends. Both are required to effectively use AI to prepare for the future.

Don't Fall for Trend Traps

Staying on top of industry trends is essential but chasing them blindly is dangerous.

The technology landscape is filled with buzzwords, vendor hype, and "can't-miss" innovations that disappear almost as quickly as they arrived. As a Predictable Leader, your responsibility is to stay informed but also stay grounded.

You are not a trend follower. You are a trend filter.

CHAPTER 7   RULE #7—PREPARE FOR THE FUTURE

Predictability applies change deliberately, based on what your business, your team, and your operations actually need. Many organizations fall into the trap of adopting the latest technologies not because they solve a real problem, but because they fear falling behind.

Some trends are real breakthroughs. Others are noise. The trick is knowing which is which.

Consider:

- Blockchain was once proposed as the solution to everything from supply chain to HR systems. In most organizations, it never left the pilot stage.

- Metaverse meetings were hailed as the next evolution of workplace collaboration. Then everyone went back to Zoom.

- Countless "AI-powered" platforms promise transformation, but without clarity on what's being transformed or why.

As a leader, your credibility is tied to your discernment. You must evaluate new technologies through the lens of business value, not how cool they are. Ask:

- Does this solve a pain point we already know exists?
- Does it align with our roadmap, people, and goals?
- Will the time and cost to implement it result in measurable value?

This is where AI can also help. Instead of using AI to chase trends, use it to *analyze them*:

- Summarize the latest industry developments.
- Compare new tools to your current stack.
- Extract practical use cases from large vendor announcements.

CHAPTER 7   RULE #7—PREPARE FOR THE FUTURE

When used wisely, AI becomes your signal booster and your noise filter.

Being prepared for the future means knowing which futures are worth preparing for.

> **⋅[AI]⋅ PROMPT THE AI—SPOT THE SIGNAL IN THE NOISE**
>
> Use AI to help you separate trend from trap. Try prompts like
>
> - *"Summarize the current tech trends in [industry], and identify which are likely short-term hype."*
>
> - *"Compare [Vendor's New Tech] to existing tools in [your environment]. What's truly different or valuable?"*
>
> - *"Give examples of technology trends that failed to deliver business value in the past five years."*
>
> - *"Which 2025 AI tools are most likely to be deprecated or replaced in the next 18 months?"*
>
> - *"Which industry trends have been overhyped in enterprise IT, and what lessons can be learned?"*
>
> Let the AI do the heavy reading so you can focus on the heavy thinking.

Build a Roadmap

Progress and transformation might seem inevitable, but it doesn't reach a successful conclusion by accident. Deliberate planning is required. This requires every team to have a roadmap. Regardless of team size, everyone on that team should know to a person what they are working toward and where they are going.

A roadmap commits you to forward momentum. While progress in IT can feel constant, unmanaged progress is often directionless.

CHAPTER 7   RULE #7—PREPARE FOR THE FUTURE

A roadmap gives form to intention. It provides visibility, accountability, and alignment. In the Age of AI, a roadmap that incorporates both human and machine strengths becomes your most strategic leadership tool.

Each roadmap should be more than just a list of technical upgrades. It should reflect the operational trust you've built (Track 1) and the strategic preparation you've led (Track 2). When you build your roadmap around the foundation of the Rules, you give every action context and every initiative purpose.

Roadmaps don't need to be grandiose in concept and scale. However, they should have a foundation based on the previous Rules and the Tracks they represent:

Roadmap Foundations by Rule

Rule	Focus Area	Roadmap Input
Rule #1—Operations Should Be Boring	Support and Customer Experience	Identify gaps in uptime, service reliability, performance friction
Rule #2—Measure What Matters	Metrics and KPIs	Highlight recurring problems through AI-driven analysis
Rule #3—Develop Your Team	Skills and Accountability	Prioritize team development, AI upskilling, and role clarity
Rule #4—Know What It Costs	Financial Discipline	Budget remediation, contract renegotiation, cost optimization
Rule #5—Communication Is Essential	Transparency and Change	Build trust through clear stakeholder engagement
Rule #6—Be a Trusted Partner	Strategic Alignment	Ensure roadmap goals reflect business priorities
AI Transformation (Integrated)	Machine/Human Synergy	Embed AI tool adoption across all initiatives

163

CHAPTER 7   RULE #7—PREPARE FOR THE FUTURE

> **TAKE A RISK—BE A SKEPTIC WITH A STRATEGY**
>
> The risk isn't ignoring the latest trend. The real risk is adopting it in your roadmap without purpose.
>
> Vendors will pitch breakthroughs. Influencers will shout disruption. The Predictable Leader knows that not every shiny object deserves investment or attention. Be brave enough to say, *"Not now."*
>
> This doesn't mean you're out of touch. It means you're selective, grounded, and focused on what works. The boldest move isn't always adoption but can be simple discernment.
>
> Take the risk of saying no, or not yet. Take the risk of asking hard questions. Take the risk of protecting your roadmap from distractions disguised as innovation.

Define a Finish Line

Roadmaps, and the associated goals within the roadmap, must be **time-constrained**. As we discussed previously, action items without a target date are merely suggestions. If you present your roadmap without any time-lines for delivery, it will not be seen as reliable. In fact, it will be considered vaporware by most of your peers and leaders within the business.

Each goal within your roadmap should have both a start date and a finish date. This lets your team, your customers, your partners, and your business know when you intend to start working on the goal, and when you expect to complete it. Doing so sets very specific expectations with your team (vendors included) for when engagement and delivery is required.

Form 7.1—Simple Roadmap Table will give you an idea of how this can be tracked.

CHAPTER 7   RULE #7—PREPARE FOR THE FUTURE

> **TAKE A RISK—MAKE YOUR ROADMAP PUBLIC**
>
> The most Predictable roadmaps aren't hidden in team folders. They're shared, socialized, and referenced constantly. The risk? Accountability. The reward? Credibility.
>
> Make your roadmap visible—to your team, your partners, and your leadership. The more eyes on it, the more trust in your progress.

Include Your Extended Team

The most effective roadmaps are forged through collaboration. This includes

- **Your internal teams**: Each function should contribute its perspective. What's broken? What's working? What's coming?

- **Vendors and service providers**: Ask them where your contracts can flex. What roadmap items could be accelerated with better tooling or training? Where are they adding AI features?

- **Business peers**: Use IT steering committees or informal syncs to ask what's missing. What are their biggest pain points? What's coming next quarter?

- **AI itself**: Your AI tools can help sequence priorities, flag gaps, and even recommend new roadmap items based on historical patterns.

CHAPTER 7   RULE #7—PREPARE FOR THE FUTURE

> **[AI] PROMPT THE AI—ROADMAP READINESS SCAN**
>
> Upload your current roadmap (or create a simple one) and prompt
>
> "Based on this roadmap, what gaps exist in team capability, business alignment, or timeline realism?"
>
> "What initiatives could be sequenced more effectively?"
>
> "Which efforts are most suitable for automation or AI augmentation?"

From Experiment to Operational Reality

Preparing for the future doesn't mean chasing every shiny object, but it does mean testing what might give you an edge *before* it's mainstream.

My teams didn't wake up one morning and "adopt AI." We tested, refined, and operationalized it where it solved real problems. Since 2015, my teams have used **IBM Watson** for text pattern recognition, like surfacing trends in support tickets that humans would miss. We worked with data intelligence teams in the deployment of **Splunk ITSI** for incident correlation and anomaly detection that got smarter the more we fed it. We embedded AI-driven security engines like **ZScaler** and **Palo Alto Networks** to flag threats in real time that would bury a human analyst. And recently, tools like **CoPilot** and **ChatGPT** have helped multiple teams across IT and the business to analyze trends and sharpen communication.

Did these tools solve everything? Of course not. But each one added a layer of predictability and taught us exactly where the human edge still matters most.

That's what makes your Ops future-ready: you run safe experiments, capture the wins, and protect your teams from being surprised by what's next.

Real World Example—From On-Prem to Cloud-First

Another great example of Predictable foresight in my career came when I led our shift to a "Cloud-First" approach. Our dependence on physical infrastructure meant that transformation and expansion were unpredictable undertakings, so we set out to fix that. We started with simple essentials such as moving our VPN solution from physical endpoints in our data centers to virtual appliances in Google's Cloud. We also replaced our on-prem monitoring systems with SaaS tools like LogicMonitor. This was the beginning of the effort and certainly not the full extent.

Each move was intentional, not merely a lift-and-shift, with each being a step toward reducing our physical infrastructure footprint. By migrating these workloads to the cloud, we gave ourselves the ability to expand our footprint to new locations, anywhere in the world, through code.

What used to take weeks or months such as ordering hardware, waiting on lead times, dealing with physical installs, and so forth became a series of automated button clicks. Ramp-up, ramp-down, and expansion all became Predictable.

Our future stopped being extended guesswork and started becoming automated, repeatable reality. That's the power of preparing for the future before it arrives: your team doesn't just react. They **LEAD**.

CHAPTER 7   RULE #7—PREPARE FOR THE FUTURE

AI Transformation
Stepping into the Future of IT Operations

The Predictable Leader has built the foundation of Predictable Ops across the 2 Tracks and 7 Rules, and is prepared for what comes next. One then asks, what next steps do we take? This is where we take a look at what we have learned so far, to further refine our roadmap to step into the future of IT with AI.

This book has made the assumption that at the most basic, you're already using Generative AI. Or if you weren't already, the **Prompt the AI** sections would have steered you in that direction. When you think of what you have prepared to lead the transformation, think of the following sample data points you have developed and how they flow into organizational decisions about AI:

Topic	AI Transformation
Support Availability	Agentic AI
KPIs and Metrics	AI/ML Algorithms (AIOps)
Team Accountability	AI-Enabled Collaboration Tools
Budget Forecasting	AIOps, Generative AI, RAG
Process Workflows	AI Automation Tools
Customer Communication	Agentic AI, AIOps, Generative AI
Partner Alignment	Generative AI, RAG Integration

CHAPTER 7   RULE #7—PREPARE FOR THE FUTURE

As the Predictable Leader, your job is to guide the transformation into AI-augmented operations, starting with what matters most. The roadmap you've followed through these Rules should highlight where your company, your partners, and your team will gain the most value from AI.

Not sure where to begin? ***Appendix A: AI, ML, and Deep Learning Tools for the Predictable Ops Journey*** provides a practical table to help you correlate your operational focus areas with the right AI capabilities.

Chapter Summary—Rule #7—Prepare for the Future

This Rule strengthens **Track 2—Preparation and Foresight** by making readiness a habit, not a hope. Stay curious, test early, deliver steadily: that's how Predictable Ops lead the future instead of getting run over by it.

A Predictable Leader does more than just keep today's operations stable. They keep their teams ready for what's next. That means staying up-to-date and modern, but not chasing every shiny new tool just because it's trending.

You plug into the future of your business by scanning for what will truly shift your cost, risk, and performance curves. AI is your bridge between these trends and real business value, helping you test assumptions, spot gaps, and forecast what legacy systems can't handle tomorrow.

You don't fall for trend traps or vendor buzzwords that promise "future-proofing" without substance. Instead, you build a clear, practical roadmap that sets direction and pace, and you run experiments that turn ideas into operational reality before the market leaves you behind.

Most important, you do this all without putting today's trust at risk. The future of Predictable Ops isn't just about being ready when change comes, it's about making the next platform shift boring, stable, and safe enough that your business follows you there willingly.

CHAPTER 8

Rule #8—Be Decisive

*Many leaders float on a breeze, offering little direction to their team. The Predictable Leader does not shift their stance based on what's forced upon them, nor do they consistently fail to provide clarity or act without conviction. Decisive leaders don't just accept their mistakes, they **own them**, correct them, and restore Predictability as fast as possible.*

Be Decisive. It's the final Rule because it's the one that makes all the others real. This Rule is where **Operational Trust** and **Preparation and Foresight** converge. All the trust you've built and all the signals you've gathered mean nothing if you freeze. Decisiveness turns preparation into action.

You can build Operational Trust. You can prepare for the future. But none of that means anything if you hesitate when it matters most.

Predictable Ops depend on leadership that doesn't drift on the breeze or cling to bad decisions. They depend on a leader who sets the direction, corrects the course when reality changes, and stands their ground when the stakes demand it.

In the Age of AI, this truth hasn't changed, it's just been amplified. AI can

- Forecast
- Analyze
- Recommend
- Automate

CHAPTER 8   RULE #8—BE DECISIVE

But it will never, and must never, decide for you. That responsibility will always rest on your shoulders.

This is the culmination of what it means to be a Predictable Leader. To be blunt, **every previous Rule will collapse** under the weight of indecision. Without clear direction and conviction, measurement becomes noise, team development loses focus, and AI becomes chaos disguised as innovation.

Predictable Ops isn't magic. It's a choice, and that choice is yours to make, every time.

Chapter Topics—Be Decisive

- Connect the Predictable Ops Rules
- Setting the Direction
- Course Correcting
- Standing Your Ground
- The Decisive Loop
- Being Decisive in the Age of AI
- Take a Risk and Prompt the AI
- Chapter Summary

Connect the Predictable Ops Rules

Predictable Ops is more than a collection of ideas. Predictable Ops is an operating system. Everything you've built in the last seven Rules comes to life here.

CHAPTER 8   RULE #8—BE DECISIVE

- Track 1 gave you Operational Trust: clear expectations, healthy accountability, transparent communication.
- Track 2 gave you Preparation and Foresight: realistic forecasting, cost discipline, and the courage to spot what's coming before it arrives.

But none of it means a thing if you freeze when the moment demands a call.

Decisiveness is what transforms your data, tools, and trust into real Predictable Ops. When you act clearly, visibly, and quickly, you show your team and your business that your operations aren't just stable by luck. They're stable because you make them that way. Every good process needs a human willing to say, *"Go."*

And like any system, its parts rely on each other. Decisiveness is the glue that keeps them working in harmony.

- You can't measure what matters (Rule #2) if you can't decide what's worth tracking and what isn't.
- You can't develop your team (Rule #3) if you can't choose where to invest your time and trust.
- You can't communicate honestly (Rule #5) if you won't commit to a position when it matters most.
- You can't be a trusted partner (Rule #6) if you sway with every opinion and never draw a line.
- You can't prepare for the future (Rule #7) if you never make the call to pivot, invest, or stop what's not working.
- You can't manage costs wisely (Rule #4) if you won't say no to waste and yes to what delivers value.

- And you can't build boring, stable operations (Rule #1) if you let small problems fester because you fear making tough calls.

Each of these Rules gives you the data, the relationships, the insights, and the confidence to act.

Rule #8 is where you prove you will.

When you're decisive, you make the other Rules real.

When you hesitate, you break the chain and Predictable Ops falls back into chaos.

In the Age of AI, that hesitation doesn't just stall progress. It amplifies risk, at machine speed.

Be the leader who pulls it all together. Be decisive and be Predictable.

Volumes have been written about what it means to be "decisive" in leadership. In the context of Predictable Ops, we can distill decisiveness into three core behaviors:

- **Set the Direction** – Your team needs clarity, especially as AI disrupts traditional roles and processes.

- **Course Correct Quickly** – Mistakes in logic or implementation, especially those amplified by AI, must be addressed without delay.

- **Stand Your Ground** – If your priorities are solid, defend them even when the machine, the boardroom, or the latest trend tells you otherwise.

In the age of AI, indecision is an **active risk multiplier**. Decisive leaders mitigate this by acting with intention, adjusting with purpose, and never outsourcing responsibility to algorithms.

Setting the Direction

Your team looks to you for answers to two questions, whether they say it or not:

"Where are we going?" and **"Why am I here?"**

In Predictable Ops, *Setting the Direction* means you take all the information you've built: your metrics (Rule #2), your team's capabilities (Rule #3), your financial boundaries (Rule #4), your trusted partnerships (Rule #6), and your readiness for what's next (Rule #7), and turn it into clear priorities your people can act on.

You need to give your team a North Star when the day-to-day feels chaotic. It's more than just a grand strategy that never changes. That is doomed to failure. When people know their purpose and know where they are headed, the white noise of life gets filtered out.

In the Age of AI, this has never mattered more — because now, the noise is louder, the inputs are endless, and the machine can spit out a thousand "suggestions" in seconds.

Without direction, your team will drown in possibility.

Without priorities, your AI systems will optimize for everything—which means they'll optimize nothing.

And when you fail to set direction, your people start to drift. The question **"Why am I here?"** becomes harder to answer.

A Predictable Leader makes it obvious:

- **Here's what matters now.**
- **Here's how you contribute.**
- **Here's how we'll know we're winning.**

YOU DON'T FREEZE when the context shifts as the data changes, the business pivots, or the AI insights reveal a new risk.

You realign the direction. You say, **"Now, this is what matters."** You keep your team moving forward, together.

Setting the direction is not a once-a-year PowerPoint slide. It's a daily act of clarity.

One that only you can deliver. Not the machine.

Course Correcting

How many times have we all heard the phrase, "You broke it, you bought it." We hear it on TV shows, we see it in print, we've had it told to us in a professional setting. The implication is often that when you make a mistake, you are stuck with it. In other words, you must accept the mess you created. Therefore, "If you own your mistakes, then you can be depended upon to live with the consequences."

Is this not Predictable? Yes, but it's **Predictably Bad**.

Remember, your mistakes affect more than just you and your team. A mistake left to fester creates institutional and lasting rot. If it's not working, fix it! Do not fall into the trap of consistency for its own sake.

Let's take a step back and look at the philosophy of some learned societies:

> "If you get on the wrong train, get off at the next station—the longer you stay on, the more expensive the return trip will be."
>
> — Japanese proverb

> "No matter how far you have gone down a wrong road, turn back."
>
> — Turkish proverb

These proverbs highlight an essential truth: if you can't recognize when your direction is wrong, every step forward becomes more costly. The Predictable Leader sees misdirection early and course corrects **quickly**. This is done not to protect ego, but to protect outcomes.

This is especially critical in today's AI-driven environment. AI systems are trained on data, guided by metrics, and shaped by assumptions. If those assumptions are wrong, or if your initial use of AI leads to poor outcomes, **doubling down is not discipline, it's dysfunction at machine speed**.

The danger with AI is that it makes mistakes seem objective. You may feel less urgency to course correct because "the model said so." That's why decisiveness matters more than ever. You must be willing to intervene, override, retrain, or redirect the system. AI doesn't absolve you from leadership. It demands it.

Amazon has a Core Value that states, *"Be Right, A Lot."* I find this phrasing particularly powerful. It's decisive, but not draconian. It doesn't say "Always be right." It leaves room for **learning, correction, and iteration**. If you weren't right the first time, then be right with the fix. Be right with what you learned. Be right next time and the time after.

To keep things wrong, especially when they can scale as fast as AI will allow, is absurd. You must be prepared to **course correct over and over again**, because in an AI-augmented world, even small errors left unchecked can become exponentially damaging.

TAKE A RISK—OVERRIDE THE MACHINE

AI can make bad decisions look smart. The models are confident. The outputs are fast. The dashboards are polished. But just because a system produces an answer doesn't mean it's the right one.

The risk isn't in using AI, it's in assuming it can't be wrong. A decisive leader knows when to trust the system and when to hit pause. When results don't feel right, don't be afraid to step in and override.

You're not disrupting the process. You're doing your job.

AI doesn't understand context, politics, or ethics the way you do. It can amplify small mistakes into large-scale failures if left unchecked. **Letting the machine run with bad logic isn't automation. It's abdication.**

CHAPTER 8   RULE #8—BE DECISIVE

Standing Your Ground

There is nothing less Predictable than a spineless leader. When you don't defend your position, or you simply follow the crowd, or you change your decisions merely to gain favor, the detrimental effects are broad and lasting. You will be seen as weak, indecisive, and a poor leader. No one will be able to trust your decisions when you don't have the strength of conviction to stand behind them.

Does this fly in the face of being willing to Course Correct? Absolutely not. Course corrections imply owning the mistake, identifying the appropriate actions to take, and then executing on that plan. You stand your ground by defending the **solution**, not the **mistake**. Conversely, standing by your error is merely obstinance. It is your responsibility as a leader to know the difference.

This distinction becomes especially important in the age of AI.

You will increasingly encounter recommendations, automations, or decisions generated by machine logic. Many of these will be useful but some will be flawed, context-blind, or outright risky. **Standing your ground may mean pushing back against what the system suggests.** It may mean pausing automation, overruling an AI-based decision, or delaying a rollout based on your judgment. That's not resistance to progress, it's the application of wisdom.

Predictable leadership doesn't follow AI blindly. It questions, validates, and, when needed, says "no."

> **·{AI}· PROMPT THE AI—TEST YOUR DECISIONS**

Model the impact of a decision before you implement it. Upload a project summary, team structure, or service plan and prompt the AI with

- "Do you see any blind spots in this decision?"

- "Based on previous implementations, can you see where this could fail?"
- "What conflicts in other departments can I anticipate?"

AI can help surface tradeoffs, snowballing effects, and stakeholder friction. But remember, its suggestions are just *signals*, not mandates.

Use AI to **sharpen your thinking—not substitute it.** Leadership begins where the prompt ends.

Real World Example—The Rules and the Tracks in Action

Many years ago, I led the technical team that was implementing a Reverse Logistics system. At the time, I was an IT leader, a project principal, and an operations lead, so it fell to me to deliver on multiple aspects of the project.

The most critical aspect of the project, besides the fact that the solution needed to work flawlessly, was that it had a hard delivery date during the holiday shopping season, which began in late November and continued on through the end of year holidays.

Reverse Logistics includes many disciplines, but in this case the solution dealt with the return of products from customers. The system we were implementing dealt with the receipt of the returned products, the testing of the returned products, determining the disposition of the products, and then ultimately deciding where the returned product would end up: on the scrap heap or refurbished. The ability to make this decision meant many millions of dollars to the company.

When I look back, every Rule was there. We built a repeatable process (Rule #1). We empowered our technicians to test and decide (Rule #2). We filled skill gaps with contractors and vendors (Rule #3). We stayed brutally

CHAPTER 8   RULE #8—BE DECISIVE

aware of the investment and ROI (Rule #4). We kept stakeholders informed and risks visible (Rule #5). We built strong relationships and aligned deliverables (Rule #6). We were ready for Day 1 and Day 100 including vendor changes and compliance risks (Rule #7).

What made it work was our willingness to make hard calls when the unexpected happened. Setting the direction, course correcting in real time, and standing our ground turned our Predictable Ops playbook into reality. We delivered a system, and we delivered trust, foresight, and decisive action, right when it mattered most.

A Predictable Ops plan means nothing without a Predictable Leader willing to pull the trigger.

 Real World Example—The Cost of Indecision

Just as a Predictable leader can have wins, ignoring the Predictable Ops Tracks invites painful losses.

I've seen what happens when you wait too long to act. Years ago, we knew a vendor relationship was crumbling. Performance was slipping, early warnings were clear, and the costs were creeping up. But I hesitated, waiting for a perfect exit plan that never materialized on its own. The longer I waited, the more leverage we lost and the more it cost us in productivity and customer satisfaction. By the time I finally made the call to pivot, our trust with the business was already eroded because they'd been living with the pain while I kept "thinking it through."

That's the hidden price of indecision: it compounds while you're standing still, and it costs you more than money. It costs you credibility. It's a lesson that every Predictable Leader eventually learns: there is no perfect moment.

That's the Predictable Ops way: **Decide, act, adapt** before small risks become chaos.

The Decisive Loop

In Predictable Ops, no decision is final. Make the best decision for right now, until new facts say otherwise.

Decisiveness is about knowing how to move when you don't have perfect information, and adjust fast when reality changes. A Predictable Leader makes this repeatable by using a simple mental model: **the Decisive Loop** (Figure 8-1).

Here's how it works:

1. Sense

Trust your signals. Both human and machine. Watch for early warnings in your metrics, AI models, frontline feedback, and your own experience. Good data is your radar; your job is to keep it clean, relevant, and flowing.

2. Decide

Don't get stuck waiting for 100% certainty because you'll never have it. Use the trust you've built in your team and tools to pick a path. Make the trade-offs visible: what you're optimizing for, what you're willing to risk, and what success looks like.

3. Act

A decision means nothing if no one acts on it. Communicate your call clearly: the what, why, and what happens next. Remove blockers. Push through the noise. Own the fallout if it doesn't go to plan.

4. Adapt

The first decision is rarely the final one. Watch what happens. Sense new signals. Adjust course before small problems compound into chaos. Keep the loop moving because that's what turns a bold decision into Predictable progress.

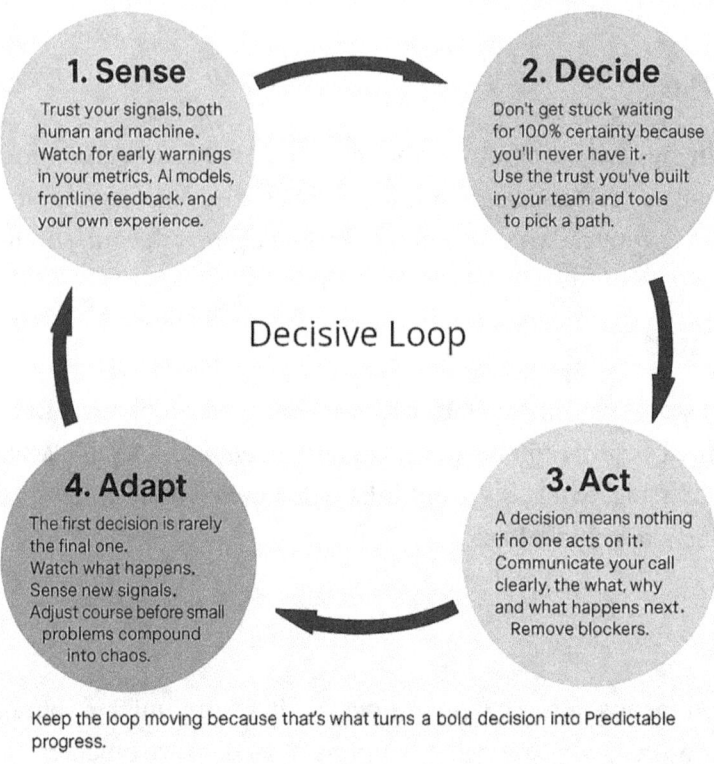

Figure 8-1. The Decisive Loop

Team-Level Decisiveness

And remember, this loop doesn't just live in your head. Predictable Ops means your frontline people know when to run it, too.

Being decisive isn't a solo act. Your frontline leads and technical SMEs need to know when they can and should act without waiting for you. That means clear decision guardrails: when to escalate, when to course-correct, when to override the process.

If your team waits for you to decide everything, your operations will stall the second you look away. If you show them what good decisiveness looks like by balancing risk, communicating clearly, and adjusting fast, they'll learn to trust their own judgment too. That's how Predictable Ops stays steady, even when you're not in the room.

 Being Decisive in the Age of AI

The promise of AI is speed. The danger of AI is speed without judgment. AI makes our jobs faster and sometimes harder. Models can churn out forecasts, detect anomalies, and suggest options at machine speed. Unfortunately they can't weigh politics, context, or the human impact of a decision gone wrong. The risk today isn't just bad data, rather it's ignoring your own judgment when the machine feels more confident than you do.

Predictable Leaders use AI to see around corners but they override it when the corner looks like a cliff. Indecision is no longer harmless; it's a risk multiplier that runs at machine scale and speed. In the Age of AI, you don't get extra credit for waiting. You get predictable when you choose.

AI can gather inputs, analyze mountains of data, and recommend actions faster than any human ever could, but it cannot choose *what truly matters*. That responsibility will never belong to the machine.

CHAPTER 8   RULE #8—BE DECISIVE

In Predictable Ops, decisiveness means you don't let AI become an excuse for indecision.

A model might say, "This is the trend."

A dashboard might say, "This is the anomaly."

A prompt might say, "This is your best course of action."

But at the end of the day, someone must say, **"Yes. This is what we're doing."**

When you are decisive with AI:

- You **validate the insights**, but you don't accept them blindly.

- You **pressure-test recommendations** against your real-world context, politics, and constraints.

- You **act quickly**, knowing that bad assumptions scale faster when AI automates them.

- You **override the system** when your judgment tells you it's wrong.

A hesitant leader lets the machine's output drive the direction by default.

A Predictable Leader makes the machine *an amplifier* for their clarity—not a substitute for it.

Remember: AI is your partner, not your replacement. Its value comes from expanding what you see, not replacing what you decide.

When the stakes are high, the data is noisy, and the pressure is on to "trust the system," your team needs one thing more than a shiny new tool:

They need you to decide.

Chapter Summary: Rule #8—Be Decisive

A Predictable Leader knows that no amount of trust, foresight, or AI-powered insight matters if you freeze when it's time to act. Decisiveness is what transforms the Rules and Tracks into real outcomes and is the force that turns planning into progress and risk into predictable action.

In the Age of AI, indecision is no longer harmless. The results from feckless leadership multiplies at machine speed. Your data, models, and forecasts will surface risks and opportunities faster than ever, but they can't weigh human context, politics, or consequences. That's your job. When you hesitate, you let the system decide by default and that's not Predictable Ops, that's abdication.

Decisiveness means you know when to set the direction, when to course correct, and when to stand your ground. It means you run the Loop—Sense, Decide, Act, Adapt—every day, and you teach your teams to run it too. It means you override the machine when your judgment sees the cliff that your model doesn't.

A Predictable Ops plan means nothing without a leader willing to pull the trigger. The Rules and Tracks build the foundation but you're the one who says *"Go."* That's what makes your operations boring, trusted, and ready for whatever the next change brings.

The courage to choose is what makes Predictable Ops real.

Conclusion— Leading Predictability in an Unpredictable World

At the end of this journey, we reflect on a few key aspects. There are certain operational truths that are timeless and fundamental to success in IT Leadership. AI doesn't replace operational excellence, it will amplify its consequences. Confident, human-centered leadership augmented by powerful tools is the gateway to leadership in the era of AI.

Now let's rephrase the importance of the 8 Rules, from the perspective of a Predictable Leader who has taken the journey.

Rule #1: Operations Should Be Boring

True leaders don't chase chaos. Rather, they build calm. Predictability earns trust, and stability is the launchpad for innovation. When your team, your business, and your customers know what to expect, they're free to grow, not just react.

Rule #2: Measure What Matters

What gets measured gets improved. The right metrics give you clarity, direction, and truth. They shine a light on where to press forward and where to stop and fix what's holding you back.

Rule #3: Develop Your Team

No AI tool can outperform a team that's growing, learning, and building momentum. Your team is your legacy, so invest in them and they'll become your greatest strategic advantage.

Rule #4: Know What It Costs

Accountability starts with awareness. When you understand the cost of your services, you speak the language of business. Predictable leaders win by knowing whenever possible, not by guessing.

Rule #5: Communication Is Essential

You can't lead in silence. Predictable communication builds alignment, manages expectations, and keeps people grounded even when everything else is changing.

Rule #6: Be a Trusted Partner

The strongest leaders are more than just operators. They're also staunch collaborators. They show up early, stay engaged, and become the people others count on when the stakes are highest.

Rule #7: Prepare for the Future

The future won't wait. Great leaders anticipate change and position their teams to thrive in it. Predictability is about staying ready.

Rule #8: Be Decisive

AI can suggest. Data can inform. But only people can lead. Decisive leaders act with courage, course correct with clarity, and never shy away from doing what's right even when it's hard.

Here is how these Rules all work together in harmony, to create the foundation for Predictable Ops.

Track One: Stability, Trust, and Communication

These Rules focus on *building trust through consistency, support, and leadership presence.*

- **Rule #1 – Operations Should Be Boring**

    Build stable, quiet, documented operations. Eliminate chaos before adding complexity.

- **Rule #3 – Develop Your Team**

    Invest in growth, skills, and accountability. Predictable Ops requires reliable people.

- **Rule #5 – Communication Is Essential**

    Communicate with clarity, timing, and empathy especially in moments of change.

- **Rule #6 – Be a Trusted Partner**

    Partnership is earned. Be visible, collaborative, and reliable especially when AI transformation begins.

Track Two: Preparation and Insight

These Rules focus on *building awareness, measurement, and foresight*—the internal foundations of Predictable Leadership.

- **Rule #2 – Measure What Matters**
- Learn to separate meaningful metrics from noise. Avoid KPI traps and vanity dashboards.
- **Rule #4 – Know What It Costs**
- Gain clarity into financial, operational, and opportunity costs. Build transparency and fiscal literacy.
- **Rule #7 – Prepare for the Future**
- Stay informed on technology and business trends. Lead through change, not in reaction to it.

Final Convergence: Leading with Confidence

- **Rule #8 – Be Decisive**
- This is where both tracks converge. All your preparation and trust-building culminate in *confident, timely decision-making* including when to lean into AI and when to override it.

AI Transformation—Get Started

AI-driven IT transformation only works if it's built on timeless Predictable truths: measurement, team development, communication, partnership, preparation, and decisiveness.

CONCLUSION—LEADING PREDICTABILITY IN AN UNPREDICTABLE WORLD

You can apply these lessons to improve your operations today even without touching AI. But make no mistake: the AI transformation is already underway, and as a leader, **you must be the one to chart the path forward**.

You've seen how the two Tracks, Operational Trust and Preparation & Foresight, work together to build Predictable Ops. Alone, they keep your services stable and your plans realistic. But together, they do something even more important in the Age of AI: they create the guardrails that keep machine-driven insights from becoming machine-driven chaos.

Track 1 ensures your team knows what's true, what's trusted, and who's accountable for what happens next. Track 2 ensures you're watching the horizon for the trends, costs, and blind spots that AI can surface faster than you could ever do manually.

But neither Track is enough on its own. It's your willingness to be decisive and to connect trust and foresight with clear action that will turn AI into an advantage. Data is everywhere now; insights are cheap. The value is in having the human judgment to steer what you see into predictable outcomes.

That's the real AI transformation: a Predictable Leader using trust, foresight, and courage to make the call even when the machine says, "Wait for more data."

Review the AI, ML, and Deep Learning tools that are available in **Appendix A**. The list is not comprehensive by any means, but it is a useful guide for the journey ahead. Learn which tools meet your business needs, be the first to lead the charge, apply the tools to your data and your processes. You are the agent of change.

AI does not replace operational excellence. It **amplifies** its consequences. When you build a strong operations culture rooted in rigor, discipline, decisive leadership, and clear communication, **AI will multiply your impact.** It will help you scale, accelerate, and sharpen what you're already doing well.

If you try to implement AI to fix a broken foundation, it will only accelerate your collapse. **AI will not fix what is already broken.** It will expose it both brutally and immediately.

Let that be your advantage. Embrace the power of AI to reveal what needs attention. Then fix it yourself like a Predictable Leader should. AI will not be a transformative tool if not governed by confident, human-centered leadership. Predictable Ops is the tool to transform you into that leader.

You are the Predictable Leader. At the end of the day, AI is just another tool on your Predictable Leader's belt, like a carpenter's hammer and saw. Tools multiply your skill, but they don't replace your craft.

Final Words

I wish I had known much of this 20+ years ago. A solid framework to build from is invaluable and an accelerant. Now you have the framework you need to build your own, high functioning Predictable Ops as a Predictable Leader.

You've seen the system. You've seen what Predictable Ops really means: trust, foresight, and the courage to act when the moment demands it.

You don't need to be perfect, and you won't ever be. You need to be consistent, honest, and decisive. That's what builds trust. That's what earns the right to lead. You've learned how to spot the signals, course-correct the spend, develop your people, and keep the machine from running you instead of the other way around.

You are ready to lead Predictable Ops because you know you'll never stop learning how to do it better. You're ready for the transformation to come.

Predictable Ops Is Human, Not Static

It's easy to think of Predictable Ops as just a checklist of stable systems, regular maintenance windows, and tools that spot problems faster than humans ever could. However, that's only half the story.

Predictable Ops is boring on purpose because it's the humans behind it who make it so. It's your trust in the team, your accountability when things go sideways, and your decisiveness when the information changes that keep the system alive and evolving.

It's an operating system that adapts every time you do. The better you teach your people to sense, decide, act, and adapt, the more predictable your operations become even when you're not in the room.

Reflection on the Future

The future will never stop testing your predictability. Budgets will tighten, platforms will age out, and AI tools will multiply your speed and your risk at the same time.

New trends will hit before you feel ready, but that's the point. Predictable Ops isn't about building a system cast in concrete. It's about building a system that changes safely, steadily, and visibly, because you and your team are paying attention.

You can't future-proof your tech stack forever, so future-proof your trust by staying honest, consistent, and ready to override the machine when logic breaks down.

Call to Action

When the next incident hits, the next vendor surprises you, the next big cost spike or AI blind spot shows up, don't wait for the "perfect plan."

CONCLUSION—LEADING PREDICTABILITY IN AN UNPREDICTABLE WORLD

Have a sense of what's happening. Quickly determine what matters in the moment. Act fast before the small risks become chaos. Show your people that Predictable Ops isn't just about what they do, it's about how you lead when everything else feels uncertain.

The next crisis is coming. The next transformation is already taking shape. But Predictable Ops will be ready, because you are.

Predictable Ops Field Guide

Sample Prompts: This Field Guide is your playbook for putting Predictable Ops into action, one decision, one conversation, and one system improvement at a time.

Each page gives you quick lessons, real-world pitfalls, practical AI prompts, and a *Try It This Week* action you can use right now.

Every entry connects back to the two major Tracks, **Operational Trust** or **Preparation and Foresight**, so you see how each Rule strengthens your system, not just your next project.

Keep this guide visible. Review it with your team. Return to it every time the landscape shifts or you need to get your operations back to boring, stable, and trusted.

Predictable Ops is a practice you lead every day.

Rule #1: Operations Should Be Boring

Key Lessons:
- Stability and calm are the goal, not chaos.
- Reliable processes and clear documentation replace heroics.
- You build trust when services work consistently and surprises are rare.
- Predictable Ops means services are resilient *enough*—not overbuilt or underbuilt.
- Right-size availability, clustering, and geo-redundancy to match business impact.

Quick Wins:
- Identify your top three recurring service failures. Fix root causes instead of firefighting.
- Review and update your runbooks. Make sure they're accurate, visible, and used.
- Track repeat incidents. If it happens twice, it deserves a permanent fix.

PREDICTABLE OPS FIELD GUIDE

Pitfalls to Watch:

- Rewarding "hero" behavior instead of root-cause elimination.
- Letting technical debt grow because "it's working for now."
- Assuming boring means stagnant—stable Ops frees you to innovate, not stand still.

Prompt the AI:

- "Analyze our incident logs for repeat failures. What are the top five?"
- "Summarize trends in our service complaints. Where are we patching instead of fixing?"

Try It This Week:

Pick one "firefighting" area you've been fixing over and over, and commit to a single root cause fix. Start boring, stay boring.

Pick one critical service. Document its current availability design. Is it over- or under-engineered for its business impact? Use that snapshot to set expectations and right-size your investment

Track Lens:

Track 1—Stability, Trust, and Communication:

Predictability starts here. Stable, calm operations earn trust and free your team to focus on what's next instead of constantly fighting fires.

Rule #2: Measure What Matters

Key Lessons:
- Good metrics reveal reality. Bad metrics hide it.
- You don't need more dashboards. You need better questions.
- Align measurement to outcomes, not activity. Metrics should help you decide, not just report.

Quick Wins:
- Review your top five KPIs. Do they reflect *performance* or just *busyness*?
- Ask stakeholders what they wish they could see, and why it matters.
- Audit one dashboard: What's useful? What's vanity?

Pitfalls to Watch:
- Tracking everything equally and learning nothing.
- Letting reporting become performance theater.
- Using metrics to justify past decisions instead of driving better ones.

Prompt the AI:
- "Review these KPIs. Which ones align with business outcomes?"
- "Summarize our key dashboard metrics. What's useful and what's noise?"

Try It This Week:

Pick one dashboard you manage. Remove a vanity metric, clarify one ambiguous one, and add one stakeholder-aligned metric that helps drive action.

Track Lens:

Track 2—Preparation and Foresight:

Good measurement is the foundation of foresight. You can't plan ahead or spot trends if you don't know what's true today.

Rule #3: Develop Your Team

Key Lessons:
- A Predictable Leader grows people, not just skills. Trust, accountability, and adaptability come with it.
- Your team must evolve alongside your technology and AI initiatives.
- Transparency about strengths, gaps, and upskilling keeps the entire org healthy.

Quick Wins:
- Build or refresh your Team Skills Matrix. Make strengths and gaps visible.
- Pair senior staff with juniors on stretch projects to build real experience.
- Openly discuss new AI tools and skills. Don't let fear fill the silence.

Pitfalls to Watch:
- Hoarding knowledge with "indispensable heroes."
- Letting recurring mistakes slide without coaching.
- Failing to hire ahead of known capability gaps.

Prompt the AI:
- "Analyze this skills matrix. Where do we risk single points of failure?"
- "Spot accountability trends in this project tracker. Who constantly misses deadlines?"
- "Recommend a training roadmap based on our upcoming AI initiatives."

PREDICTABLE OPS FIELD GUIDE

Try It This Week:

Schedule one 30-minute review with your leads to map current skills and name the biggest gap. Commit to a plan to close or hire for it. Don't just log it and forget it.

Track Lens:

Track 1—Stability, Trust, and Communication:

Strong, skilled people make operations predictable, because they know what's expected, hold each other accountable, and grow together.

Rule #4: Know What It Costs

Key Lessons:
- Cost surprises are the fastest way to lose operational trust.
- Budget forecasting means seeing spend drivers early, not just recording them after the fact.
- Challenge vendor assumptions before they become your reality.
- Resiliency isn't free. Every extra layer (clustering, failover, geo-redundancy) carries a cost that must match the risk.

Quick Wins:
- Identify your top three biggest vendor renewals this year. Pull real usage and see if your forecast still holds.
- Run a "worst case" scenario: What if usage spikes? What if your vendor changes the model?
- Spot duplicate or underused licenses. Don't pay twice for what you don't need.

Pitfalls to Watch:
- Blindly trusting a vendor's "guaranteed savings" pitch.
- Rolling last year's budget forward without challenging stale assumptions.
- Letting cost forecasting live only in Finance. It must live in Ops too.

Prompt the AI:
- *"Forecast spend trends based on our current usage and contracts."*
- *"Spot vendors with the biggest cost fluctuations this year."*
- *"Where could we bundle or renegotiate for savings?"*

Try It This Week:

Pick one vendor contract up for renewal. Stress-test it with AI prompts, real usage data, and a worst-case scenario before you sign again.

Run a cost snapshot on one HA system. Does the spend align with its business criticality? Pressure test the "what if it fails?" scenario.

Track Lens:

Track 2—Preparation and Foresight: Clear cost awareness keeps you ready to shape the future, not just pay for it.

Rule #5: Communication Is Essential

Key Lessons:
- Predictable Leaders don't wait to be asked. They speak first, clearly, and consistently.
- Communication sets expectations and calms the chaos when technology changes fast.
- AI tools can help you draft, summarize, and adapt messages but your candor keeps trust alive.

Quick Wins:
- Identify your core audiences: execs, frontline teams, partners, customers.
- Review one recent incident report or maintenance notice: did it answer what people really cared about?
- Use AI to test for gaps, jargon, or contradictions before you hit send.

Pitfalls to Watch:
- Overloading people with noise instead of actionable information.
- Waiting too long to communicate bad news. Trust dies in silence.
- Assuming AI-written updates mean you don't have to read every word yourself.

Prompt the AI:
- *"Draft a clear maintenance notice for both technical teams and end users."*
- *"Summarize this root cause analysis for an exec audience."*
- *"Check this status update for clarity, tone, and impact."*

Try It This Week:

Pick an upcoming planned change or risk. Communicate it before someone has to ask. Make your message clear, timely, and audience-focused.

Track Lens:

Track 1—Stability, Trust, and Communication

Clear, proactive communication is how you keep people aligned and calm, even when the tech itself changes at machine speed.

Rule #6: Be a Trusted Partner

Key Lessons:

- Operational trust alone isn't enough. You must show up for your partners when it counts.
- Credibility is built in the small moments and cemented in the big ones, like major initiatives or transformation efforts.
- A trusted partner sets clear expectations for service levels and recovery when things break.
- AI only strengthens relationships when it's deployed transparently and with clear value for everyone involved.

Quick Wins:

- Identify one key stakeholder relationship that's at risk or needs mending and schedule time to reconnect.
- Ask your partners what insights or transparency they wish they had from your Ops team.
- Draft or update a simple Service Resiliency Profile for one customer-facing system. Share it with your partners—no illusions, no surprises.
- Use AI tools *internally* first and earn trust by showing you know how to pilot before expanding impact.

Pitfalls to Watch:

- Treating AI as a magic fix for relationship problems: It will expose them, not hide them.
- Showing up only when a big deliverable is at risk. Partnership is an everyday commitment.
- Keeping insights locked in IT. Real trust comes from sharing data that helps the business succeed.

Prompt the AI:

- *"Draft a stakeholder update explaining the benefit of this initiative."*
- *"Summarize feedback trends from partners. Where are we losing trust?"*
- *"Suggest cross-department use cases for this tool that add business value."*

Try It This Week:

Have one candid conversation with a business partner about how your team's work and tooling can help *them* succeed.

Track Lens:

Track 1—Stability, Trust, and Communication

Strong partnerships grow from predictable performance—and your willingness to connect, clarify, and deliver together.

Rule #7: Prepare for the Future

Key Lessons:
- No environment stays static: Predictable Leaders watch trends, test scenarios, and evolve ahead of surprises.
- "Future-proofing" is a myth, but staying *future-ready* is within your control.
- AI is your radar, not your autopilot. Use it to scan the horizon, not to make decisions for you.

Quick Wins:
- Block time each quarter to review major tech and business trends. Don't wait for someone else to tell you what's coming.
- Compare your team's skills map to industry shifts. Are you ready for the next wave?
- Prompt AI to spot gaps in your roadmap and highlight emerging risks.

Pitfalls to Watch:
- Blindly following buzzwords. Not every trend is right for your org.
- Relying solely on vendors to "future-proof" you. The risk is yours to manage.
- Putting off upskilling until a new platform is already here.

Prompt the AI:
- "What emerging trends should we monitor over the next 12–18 months?"
- "Where does our current platform or vendor strategy fall behind peers?"
- "Suggest skills we need to build now to stay relevant as AI tools expand."

Try It This Week:

Pick one future trend you've been ignoring. Run a simple scenario: *What happens if this is real and we do nothing?*

Track Lens:

Track 2—Preparation and Foresight:

You can't steer tomorrow's risks if you're guessing where they'll hit. A Predictable Leader looks forward, tests assumptions, and adjusts early.

Rule #8: Be Decisive

Key Lessons:
- No tool, trend, or AI model will make the final call for you. That's YOUR job.
- Decisiveness turns all the trust, measurement, preparation, and partnerships you've built into action.
- Small hesitations compound at machine speed: Act, Adapt, and Teach your team to do the same.

Quick Wins:
- Identify one decision you've been delaying—make the call, share it visibly, and own it.
- Revisit your "Decisive Loop": Sense, Decide, Act, Adapt—use it on real challenges, not just big emergencies.
- Check that your team knows when they can decide on their own—and when to escalate.

Pitfalls to Watch:
- Waiting for perfect certainty. It will never come.
- Delegating the decision to the tool instead of owning it yourself.
- Not course-correcting early. Small risks ignored become chaos later.

Prompt the AI:
- "What scenarios did this forecast not account for?"
- "Summarize pros and cons for these options so I can pressure test them."
- "What early signals should I monitor if I choose this path?"

PREDICTABLE OPS FIELD GUIDE

Try It This Week:

Pick one decision you've been stuck on. Make the best call with what you know and set a date to revisit it with new signals.

Track Lens:

Both Tracks Converge:

This is where trust and foresight meet action. Decisive leaders make Predictable Ops real and keep them steady, even when the machine wants to run ahead.

APPENDIX A

AI, ML, and Deep Learning Tools for the Predictable Ops Journey

These tools represent the categories of AI technologies IT leaders should become familiar with as they adopt Predictable, AI-assisted operations.

AI Automation Tools

Automate repetitive, rules-based tasks to improve operational efficiency.

- **UiPath** – Enterprise-grade RPA (Robotic Process Automation) platform
- **Automation Anywhere** – End-to-end automation with AI integrations
- **ServiceNow Flow Designer/Virtual Agent** – Workflow automation in ITSM environments

- **Zapier** – Low-code/no-code task automation for apps and services
- **Runbooks with AI Triggers** – For example, Azure Automation, AWS Systems Manager Automation

Generative AI Tools

Used for content creation, summarization, scripting, documentation, and even chat-driven analysis.

- **ChatGPT (OpenAI)** – Text generation, coding assistance, analysis, document processing
- **GitHub Copilot** – AI-powered code assistant integrated into IDEs
- **Google Gemini** – Text, code, and productivity AI integrated across Google Workspace
- **Claude (Anthropic)** – Secure enterprise-friendly generative AI
- **Microsoft Copilot** – Embedded in Office 365 apps, Teams, and Windows
- **Jasper** – Marketing and documentation generation assistant

AI Collaboration Tools

Enhance meetings, messaging, and collaboration through AI summaries, action tracking, and scheduling.

- **Zoom AI Companion** – Meeting transcriptions, summaries, next-step suggestions

- **Microsoft Teams with Copilot** – Summarizes meetings, suggests replies, tracks tasks

- **Otter.ai** – Real-time transcription and post-meeting summarization

- **Notion AI** – Embedded AI in note-taking and documentation tools

- **Fireflies.ai** – Meeting assistant that joins calls, transcribes, and extracts action items

ML IT Data Analysis Tools

Provide insights by analyzing historical and real-time operational data.

- **Splunk with Machine Learning Toolkit** – Log and event analysis, anomaly detection

- **Dynatrace Davis AI** – AIOps engine for full-stack observability and root-cause analysis

- **PagerDuty AIOps** – Intelligent alert grouping and incident prioritization

- **Datadog Watchdog** – Detects performance regressions, errors, anomalies

- **Elastic Observability + ML** – Log and metric-based issue patterning

Deep Learning IT Tools

Advanced systems using neural networks to process complex patterns in images, voice, and large data sets.

- **AWS SageMaker** – Build, train, and deploy custom ML and DL models
- **Google Vertex AI** – Unified ML and deep learning platform
- **IBM Watson AIOps** – Deep learning-powered IT event correlation and prediction
- **H2O.ai** – Open source and enterprise AI with AutoML and deep learning
- **NVIDIA Triton Inference Server** – Serving deep learning models at scale

Retrieval-Augmented Generation (RAG) Tools

Platforms and frameworks that connect Large Language Models (LLMs) with external data sources, enabling grounded, context-aware AI responses.

- **Amazon Bedrock –** Offers native support for RAG with foundation models like Claude and Titan, integrated with vector stores and knowledge bases
- **OpenAI (with Pinecone or Azure Cognitive Search)** – Enables custom GPTs with real-time data grounding via embeddings and API-driven vector search

- **Cohere** – RAG through Embed + Rerank APIs, optimized for enterprise document and knowledge retrieval

- **LangChain** – Framework for building RAG pipelines using multiple data sources, LLMs, and vector stores (supports Python and JavaScript)

- **LlamaIndex** – Indexes and serves structured and unstructured data for RAG, simplifying LLM integration into business data workflows

- **Weaviate/Pinecone/ChromaDB** – Vector databases that store embeddings for fast similarity search, a key part of scalable RAG systems

- **ElasticSearch + NLP Plugins** – Enables lightweight RAG via document indexing and semantic search when paired with LLM APIs

Pricing and Licensing Considerations

As your organization integrates AI, ML, and deep learning tools, pricing and licensing will directly impact your adoption strategy. Predictable Ops leaders must plan for cost transparency and controlled rollout. Below are key considerations.

1. Freemium vs. Enterprise Models

- **Freemium tools** like *ChatGPT Free*, *Otter.ai*, or *Zapier* provide basic functionality—ideal for experimentation or individual use.

- **Enterprise editions** offer advanced features (API access, security, governance) but typically require team licensing or platform subscriptions.

Predictable Tip Start with low-cost tiers to test use cases. Upgrade only when value is proven.

---

2. Per-User Licensing

- Tools like *Microsoft 365 Copilot, Zoom AI Companion,* and *GitHub Copilot* often follow a **per user/month** pricing model, typically between **$10–$30 per user**.
- Even modest rollouts can accumulate significant recurring costs.

Predictable Tip Begin with a small pilot group—such as your service desk or operations team—and measure impact before scaling up.

---

3. Consumption-Based or Pay-As-You-Go Models

- Tools like *OpenAI API, Google Vertex AI,* and *AWS SageMaker* charge based on **API calls, tokens, or compute usage**.
- These models are highly scalable but **require strict cost controls**.

APPENDIX A   AI, ML, AND DEEP LEARNING TOOLS FOR THE PREDICTABLE OPS JOURNEY

Predictable Tip   Set hard usage quotas and budgeting thresholds, and work with your CloudOps or FinOps team to monitor billing.

4. Platform Lock-In and Vendor Overlap

- AI capabilities are often embedded in platforms you already use (e.g., *Teams, ServiceNow, Google Workspace*).
- Activation may require purchasing higher-tier licenses or specific add-ons.

Predictable Tip   Audit existing platforms—you may already "own" AI capabilities you haven't yet enabled.

5. Data Privacy, Retention, and AI Training

- Many tools retain interaction data for training models by default. Enterprise agreements may offer **data privacy options**, but they often come with a higher price tag.

APPENDIX A   AI, ML, AND DEEP LEARNING TOOLS FOR THE PREDICTABLE OPS JOURNEY

Predictable Tip   Before deployment, confirm

- Where your data is stored (regional sovereignty matters)
- Whether your data is used to train vendor models
- Whether opt-outs or contractual protections are available

AI Budget Starter Table

Tool Type	Example Tools	Pricing Model	Range
Generative AI	ChatGPT Pro, Microsoft Copilot	Per-user/month	Free-and-Up
AI Collaboration	Zoom AI Companion, Google Meet AI	Add-on or included	Generally based on existing license
Automation Platforms	Zapier, Make, UiPath	Tiered plans	Free-and-Up
ML/Deep Learning	OpenAI API, AWS SageMaker	Usage-based	Varies by tokens/compute
AIOps and ITSM AI	ServiceNow, Dynatrace, DataDog AI	Enterprise license	Custom/Negotiated

APPENDIX B

AI in Action

Rule #1: Operations Should Be Boring

Summary

AI enhances stability, visibility, and repeatability—core to Predictable Ops. But AI is not a fix-all. Without clean documentation and consistent operational processes, it risks amplifying dysfunction. In Rule #1, we introduce foundational AI use cases that support better tracking, analysis, and early remediation.

Where AI Applies in Rule #1

Area of Focus	AI Application Example
Support Availability	AI chatbots triage issues 24/7; virtual agents (Agentic AI) supplement thin staffing models.
Service Downtime	AI parses Form 1.1 and ticketing data to identify chronic outages and early trends.
Service Performance	AI detects performance degradation and correlates it with time-of-day or user load.

Area of Focus	AI Application Example
Documentation	AI tools auto-summarize runbooks and generate chatbot-ready how-to content.
Tool Confusion	Generative AI can explain tool usage or flag redundant/poor UX workflows.
AI-Ready Foundation	Structured inputs (runbooks, policies, diagrams) are prerequisites for AI remediation.

AI Tools You Can Use

- **ChatGPT/Copilot/Claude**: Analyze patterns from ticket exports, summarize issue logs, generate remediation steps.

- **Zoom AI Companion/Teams Copilot**: Capture meeting notes and turn them into action items for service improvement.

AIOps Platforms (e.g., Dynatrace, Moogsoft, Splunk ITSI): Auto-correlate events and alert on early warning signals.

Sample Prompts

- "Given this spreadsheet of user complaints, which services have the most repeat issues?"
- "Summarize the top causes of service downtime based on this exported ticket history."

- "Draft a chatbot response for common complaints about slow VPN connectivity."

- "What are three likely root causes of this recurring Wi-Fi complaint?"

Rule #2: Measure What Matters
Key Ideas

- Measurement is not about collecting numbers. It's about turning the right data into decisions.

- AI can parse huge volumes of telemetry, logs, and KPIs to find trends you'd miss by eye but it can't tell you what actually matters to your customers.

- Predictable Leaders use AI to detect noise vs. signal, then apply human judgment to keep the dashboards honest and focused on real business outcomes.

- Observability powered by AI makes sense only if you review it with context, curiosity, and a bias for action.

APPENDIX B   AI IN ACTION

Practical Ways to Use AI

Focus Area	How AI Helps
Parsing Metrics and KPIs	AI tools like ChatGPT, CoPilot, or industry-specific platforms (e.g., BigPanda, LogicMonitor, Dynatrace) can analyze log files, ingest dashboards, and identify trends across KPIs and telemetry data.
Dashboard Intelligence	AI can detect which dashboards are being used vs. ignored, suggest simplification, and prioritize metrics that correlate to actual business outcomes.
Root Cause Analysis	With tools like Splunk ITSI or DataDog's Watchdog, AI automatically correlates incidents, metrics, and logs to surface likely root causes.
Problem Management	AI models trained on historical issue patterns can highlight recurring problems even across systems that don't obviously relate.
Governance and Validation	AI can suggest data anomalies, alert on misleading correlations, or warn when the KPI definitions drift from reality. But humans must override when AI gets it wrong. See Rule #8 for more.

Sample Prompts

- "Parse this API log data and identify unusual response time spikes by endpoint."
- "Review these dashboards and suggest which metrics correlate best to customer satisfaction."

- "Correlate this month's ticket spikes with backend system errors—draft a summary RCA."
- "Spot any KPI definitions that have drifted from our original SLA agreement."

Rule #3: Develop Your Team

Key Ideas

- Use AI to surface hidden patterns in skills, gaps, and accountability trends.
- Make development data-driven—pair coaching with clear evidence, not just gut feel.
- Position AI as a supportive lens, not a substitute for real feedback and mentoring.

Practical Ways to Use AI

- **Skills Gap Analysis:** Upload your Team Skills Matrix and prompt AI to highlight strengths, overlaps, or gaps you may miss.
- **Accountability Trends:** Analyze task trackers to spot repeat missed deadlines, dropped handoffs, or bottlenecks.
- **Mentoring Cues:** Use AI to flag recurring mistakes so you can coach proactively.
- **Upskill Roadmap:** Generate suggestions for training or certification plans tied to real workload demands.

APPENDIX B   AI IN ACTION

Sample Prompts

- "Review this Team Skills Matrix—where do we have single points of failure?"
- "Analyze this project tracker. Are any contributors missing repeated deadlines?"
- "Which recurring mistakes should I address with coaching?"
- "What upskilling plan aligns with our next AI transformation goals?"

Rule #4: Know What It Costs

Key Ideas

- AI is an early warning system for cost surprises.
- Use AI to model spend trends, stress-test vendor assumptions, and find hidden waste.
- Combine AI forecasting with your own scenario planning to avoid budget blind spots.

Practical Ways to Use AI

- **Spend Trend Forecasts:** Prompt AI to project costs based on historical data and usage spikes.
- **Vendor Contract Analysis:** Run what-if scenarios to test cost impact of tier changes or consolidations.

- **Duplicate Spend Checks:** Use AI to compare licenses and support agreements for overlap.
- **Renewal Readiness:** Analyze upcoming renewals and prompt for savings opportunities.

Sample Prompts

- "Forecast our licensing spend for the next three years based on current growth."
- "Where are we paying twice for the same capability?"
- "Which vendor contract terms should we renegotiate?"
- "What does industry data say about our vendor mix and cost structure?"

Rule #5: Communication Is Essential
Key Ideas

- AI can boost clarity, consistency, and speed in your operational communications—but it will never replace your candor or your judgment.
- Use AI to co-write, draft, and summarize messages for different audience tiers—so people get what they need, when they need it.
- Leverage AI to keep calm, rapid updates flowing during outages, maintenance windows, and technology changes that impact your partners and customers.
- Always review what the machine drafts: AI won't know your context, politics, or tone—you do.

APPENDIX B AI IN ACTION

Practical Ways to Use AI

- **Draft Maintenance Notices:** Use generative AI to co-write clear, risk-based messages for service owners and end users.

- **Summarize Incidents Fast:** AI can help produce plain-language incident summaries that keep stakeholders calm and informed.

- **Conflict Checks for Schedules:** Feed overlapping maintenance windows into AI to flag hidden service conflicts.

- **Auto-Draft Postmortems:** Have AI generate the first draft of your RCA, then add the human nuance your partners expect.

- **Audience Tuning:** Prompt AI to adapt comms for frontline teams, execs, or customers—so nobody feels surprised or misinformed.

Sample Prompts

- *"Draft an outage notice for frontline teams and execs—two versions with the same facts but different detail."*

- *"Summarize this major incident in plain language for our quarterly business review."*

- *"Spot conflicts in these overlapping patch windows and suggest clearer scheduling options."*

- *"Refine this maintenance update for clarity, trust, and a calm tone."*

APPENDIX B   AI IN ACTION

Rule #6: Be a Trusted Partner
Key Ideas

- AI can strengthen relationships if deployed with transparency and trust.
- Use AI to deliver insights that help your business partners succeed—not just to optimize IT for its own sake.
- Build credibility by piloting AI within your own Ops team before expanding to other areas.

Practical Ways to Use AI

- **Co-Author Communications:** Draft clear status updates, risk advisories, and rollout notices with AI tools like generative text assistants.
- **Summarize Meetings:** Use AI meeting transcribers to share key points with stakeholders consistently—builds trust that nothing is hidden.
- **Analyze Relationship Health:** Upload feedback surveys or helpdesk CSAT data; prompt AI to surface patterns or signals that relationships need mending.
- **Prototype Together:** Involve business partners in co-design sessions for AI-driven processes (e.g., AI service desk, automated ticket triage).
- **Map Cross-Department AI Use Cases:** Use AI to research and compare how other departments (HR, Finance, Security, CX) can responsibly deploy AI alongside your IT initiatives.

APPENDIX B   AI IN ACTION

Sample Prompts

- "Summarize this customer feedback dataset. Where are we losing trust?"
- "Draft an email explaining how this new AI tool will improve, not replace, the work of our business team."
- "Given our current AI pilots, what partnerships across departments could we expand next?"
- "What risks should I communicate when pitching this AI solution?"

Remember:

AI won't fix trust gaps—it will magnify them. Deploy it in ways that reinforce your reputation as a dependable partner.

Rule #7: Prepare for the Future

Key Ideas

- AI expands your radar for industry and tech trends.
- Use it to compare vendor roadmaps, emerging costs, or operational impacts.
- Keep scanning for where your team's capabilities need to grow next.

Practical Ways to Use AI

- **Trend Scanning:** Prompt for trend reports in infrastructure, cloud, or security ops.

- **Scenario Testing:** Stress-test your roadmap against emerging threats or budget pressures.
- **Benchmarking:** Use AI to see how your ops strategy compares to peers.
- **Skills Forecast:** Analyze where team skills must shift to meet future AI demands.

Sample Prompts

- "What tech trends should we prepare for over the next 18 months?"
- "How might these trends impact our licensing costs?"
- "Where are we behind industry best practices?"
- "Which new AI roles should we start upskilling for?"

Rule #8: Be Decisive

Key Ideas

- AI can provide insights—but only you can make the final call.
- Use AI to test scenarios, catch blind spots, and validate your assumptions.
- Trust your judgment more than the model when the corner looks like a cliff.

APPENDIX B   AI IN ACTION

Practical Ways to Use AI

- **Scenario Forecasts:** Compare best/worst case options with real constraints.
- **Early Warning Detection:** Use anomaly detection to flag risks needing a call.
- **Decision Option Summaries:** Get AI to draft your pros and cons—then stress test them.
- **Override Cues:** Prompt AI for what its model didn't account for.

Sample Prompts

- "Summarize pros and cons of these cost-saving scenarios."
- "Where does this model miss key business risks?"
- "Draft my decision options for this failover plan."
- "What early signals should I monitor if we choose this option?"

APPENDIX C

Forms, Templates, and Tables

Form 1.1 – Service Complaints Ledger

Reported By	Complaint Type	Date of Issue	Description	Domain
Unknown	Service Downtime			
Unknown	Service Downtime			
Team	Service Downtime			
Team	Service Downtime			
Team	Service Downtime			

Reported By: The team or customer who reported the issue
Complaint Type: One of the 4+ issues described in Rule #1
Date of Issue: When the event took place
Description: A brief narrative of the issue
Domain: The IT service that was involved in the issue

APPENDIX C   FORMS, TEMPLATES, AND TABLES

Form 1.2 – Service Resiliency Profile—Template

Service Name:

For example, Customer API Gateway

Business Criticality: *Critical\High\Medium\Low*

(Brief note on why. Example: "Direct revenue impact if down.")

Availability Target (SLA):

For example, 99.9% monthly uptime

Recovery Time Objective (RTO):

How fast must it come back online after a failure? For example, 2 hours

Recovery Point Objective (RPO):

How much data loss is acceptable? For example, 15 minutes

Resiliency Design:

- *HA Clustering:* Yes/No (*If yes, where?*)

- *Failover Type:* Active-Active | Active-Passive | Manual

- *Geo-Redundancy:* Yes/No (*Regions?*)

- *Key Dependencies: For example, storage cluster, DNS failover*

Known Risks or Limitations:

Where can failure still happen? What can't be recovered automatically?

Communication Plan:

How are stakeholders notified during an outage?

Owner:

Team or SME responsible for keeping this profile accurate.

Last Reviewed:

Date + next review date.

APPENDIX C   FORMS, TEMPLATES, AND TABLES

How to use this:

- Keep it one page—the point is clarity.
- Make it a living doc in your CMDB, runbook, or shareable service portal.
- Use it to set *clear expectations* with business partners so there are no illusions about resilience levels, cost trade-offs, or recovery steps.

Table C-1. Predictable Ops Blueprint

From Chaos to Boring: The Predictable Ops Blueprint		
Maturity Level	**Human Practice**	**AI Assistance**
Level 1 – Pain Signals (Chaos)	Log complaints, track downtime, observe frustration points.	Parse tickets, group themes, visualize chronic issues
Level 2 – Documentation	Build runbooks, diagrams, policies, and ticket data.	Summarize procedures, auto-suggest fixes, power chatbots
Level 3 – Stability	Fix recurring issues, enforce process, communicate clearly	Detect early warning signs, monitor trends, trigger proactive alerts
Level 4 – Efficiency	Remove bad tools, streamline workflows, reduce friction	Automate steps, recommend optimizations, guide users contextually.
Level 5 – Predictable Ops (Boring/Calm)	Review consistently, lead transparently, build team trust	Deliver insights, scale support, keep operations boring

APPENDIX C   FORMS, TEMPLATES, AND TABLES

Table C-2. Common Ops Tools

Platform/Tool	What It's Used For
ServiceNOW	Comprehensive ITSM (ITIL) platform for incident, change, and problem management. Strong CMDB and workflow automation.
Jira Service Management	Agile-focused ticketing, issue tracking, and change control. Popular for DevOps and Ops integration.
PagerDuty	On-call scheduling, real-time incident response, and automated alerting. Helps standardize escalation paths.
Splunk ITSI	AIOps platform for real-time telemetry, correlation, anomaly detection, and root cause analysis.
Datadog/Watchdog	Infrastructure and application monitoring with AI-driven root cause suggestions. Great for cloud-heavy stacks.
BigPanda	Event correlation and noise reduction across multiple monitoring tools. Reduces alert fatigue, standardizes signals.
LogicMonitor	Full-stack observability, especially useful for hybrid cloud environments.
Microsoft Copilot/ ChatGPT	Generative AI for drafting incident updates, standardizing postmortems, or summarizing dashboards.

Form 3.1 – Team Skills Matrix

Resource	Skill 1	Skill 2	Skill 3	Skill 4	Skill 5	Skill Avg
Name	0	0	0	0	0	
Name	0	0	0	0	0	
...	0	0	0	0	0	
Name	0	0	0	0	0	
Team Avg						

Skill Ratings:

0 = No skill

1 = Rudimentary Skill

2 = Basic Skill

3 = Competent Skill

4 = Advanced Skill

5 = Expert Level Skill

Supervision and Mentoring (Skill Level):

0–2 = Requires Supervision, Training, and Mentoring

3 = No Supervision Required

4–5 = Can Train and Mentor Other Resources on the Skill

APPENDIX C   FORMS, TEMPLATES, AND TABLES

Form 3.2 – Accountability Tracker

Team Member	Task Description	Due Date	Status	Delivered On	Notes

Table C-3. *Skills Evolution Table—From Traditional IT to AI-Enabled Roles*

Traditional IT Skill	Example Role Today	How It Evolves with AI	Example New Role
Scripting and Automation	Systems Engineer	Prompt engineering for automation workflows	AI Ops Engineer
Data Analysis	Business Analyst	ML model tuning, validating AI insights	ML Ops Analyst
Monitoring and Incident Response	NOC Analyst	AI-enabled anomaly detection and root cause analysis	Reliability Engineer with ML
Runbook Development	ITIL Process Manager	Training AI agents with well-structured inputs	AI Support Agent Designer
Vendor Management	IT Vendor Manager	Analyzing spend and vendor performance with AI	AI Vendor Insights Lead
DevOps/CI-CD	DevOps Engineer	Integrating AI testing and feedback loops	AI Pipeline Engineer

Table C-4. Audience Tiers Comms Matrix

Audience Tier	What They Care About	How You Should Communicate
Executives and Sponsors	Risk, cost impact, customer trust, high-level status, big milestones	Keep it short and strategic. Highlight business impact, major risks, and actions. No deep technical noise.
Frontline Teams	Day-to-day impact, workarounds, clear tasks, who's responsible for what	Be detailed and practical. Use clear timelines, contacts, and next steps.
Partners and Vendors	Integration points, SLAs, shared responsibilities, contract obligations	Be explicit about dependencies. Show how it affects their commitments and timelines.
Customers and End Users	Direct service impact, downtime, fixes, when normal will return	Keep it simple and human. Avoid jargon. Set expectations honestly and update when things change.

APPENDIX C   FORMS, TEMPLATES, AND TABLES

Form 7.1 – Simple Roadmap Table

Roadmap Goal	Rule Link	Start Date	End Date	Owner(s)	Dependencies	AI Assistance
Automate incident routing for Tier 1 tickets	Rule #1	Aug 1	Sep 15	Service Desk Lead	Runbook readiness	CoPilot logic + chatbot integration
Identify top five recurring problems via KPI + ML analysis	Rule #2	Aug 5	Aug 30	Ops Analyst	Ticket data, dashboards	ChatGPT log parsing
Create AI onboarding workshop for engineers	Rule #3	Sep 1	Oct 15	Team Manager + L&D	AI policy approved	Internal GPT-based tools
Shrink underused software licenses by 30%	Rule #4	Aug 15	Nov 1	IT Finance	Vendor reporting access	Predictive analytics
Launch tech change notification process	Rule #5	Sep 10	Oct 1	Comms Lead	Tooling alignment	Email AI assistant

APPENDIX C   FORMS, TEMPLATES, AND TABLES

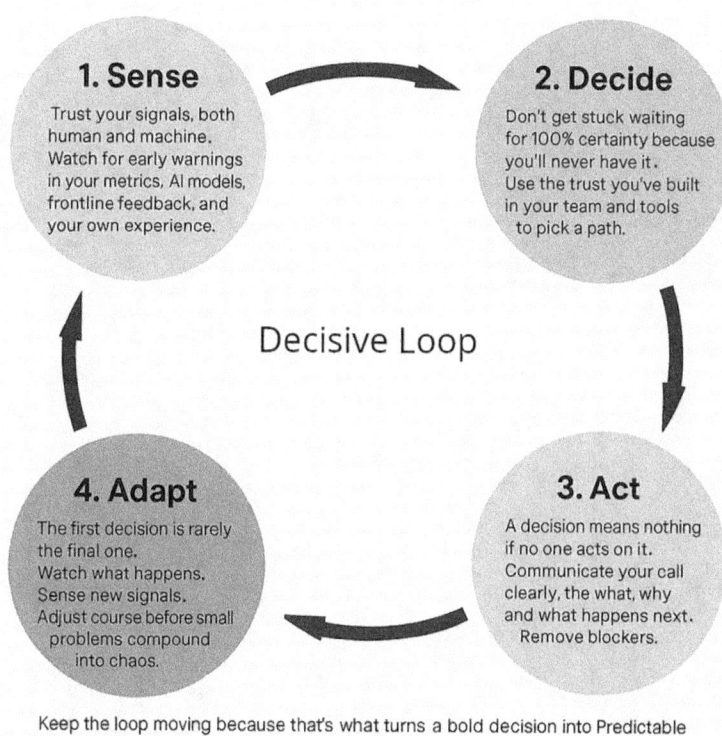

Figure C-1. *The Decisive Loop*

Index

A, B

AIOps platforms, 35, 44, 98–100, 218
Artificial intelligence (AI)
   accountability trends, 58–60
   agents, 81
   analytics tools, 98–100
   automation tools, 209
   business partners, 225, 226
   communications, 223, 224
   cost management, 222, 223
   dashboards, 43
   data analysis, 211
   decisive, 227, 228
   future proof, 168, 226, 227
   Generative AI, 98
   generative tools, 210
   ingests observability tools, 44
   IT operations, 45
   Key Performance Indicators (KPIs), 40
   measurement, 26, 219
   meetings/messaging/collaboration, 210
   ML capabilities, 72
   models, 183
   neural networks, 212
   operational process
      prompts, 218
      rules, 217
      tools, 218
   operations, 2
   pitch, 144–146
   pricing/licensing
      consideration, 213
      budget table, 216
      consumption, 214
      data privacy options, 215
      enterprise editions, 214
      freemium tools, 213
      per-user licensing, 214
      platform lock-in and vendor overlap, 215
   problem management, 50, 51
   prompts, 72
   RAG tools, 212, 213
   scenarios and vendor spend analysis, 100
   team development, 221, 222
   tools, 16
   transformation, 123–125, 190–192
   upskilling, 73, 74

INDEX

C

ChatGPT homepage, 48–50
Communication
    artificial intelligence (AI), 223, 224
    audience tiers, 107–109
    bedrock, 104
    business reviews, 111
        actions, 112
        budget variances/vendor, 111
        information, 112
        MBRs/QBRs, 112
    commitments honest, 110
    connective tissue, 103
    deadlines, 108
    delivery date, 108, 109
    high-priority outages, 117, 118
    immutable truth, 105–107
    IT policies/governance
        creation, 120
        framework, 121, 122
    leadership, 110
    maintenance schedules
        conflicts, 116
        disruptions, 113
        patching schedule, 114–116
        preventative work, 114
        proactive communication, 113
        reactive mode, 114
    overview, 188
    partners/customers, 109–111
    reviews, 107
    risk process, 111
    technology shifts, 118–120
    technology transformation, 123–125
    video conferencing team, 106
Cost management
    accountability, 84
    AI agents, 81
    AIOps platforms, 98–100
    artificial intelligence (AI), 222, 223
    assume savings
        assumptions, 89, 90
        Cloud infrastructure, 89
        hidden costs and test, 90
    budget, 84
    capital expenditures, 83
    compensation/benefits, 83
    contractual terms/conditions, 94–96
    cost increases
        budget manager, 86
        cloud platforms, 87, 88
        critical habits, 85
        licensing and support, 88, 89
        massive manual comparisons, 88
        multi-year deal, 85
        operational axiom, 84
        operational frugality, 85
        scale, 85
        vendor relationships, 85
    costs and restrictions, 94

economics, 79–81
forecast, 99–101
forewarning, 91
integration penalties, 95
operational expenses, 83
operational familiarity, 81
overview, 188
path forward, 81
preparation and foresight, 80
return on investment, 96, 97
total contract value (TCV), 95
tracking areas, 82
transparency, 82
vendors, 91–93
visibility, 83
working relationship, 81
Cybersecurity Framework (CSF), 121

D, E

Decisive leaders
artificial intelligence (AI), 227, 228
costs, 180
course corrects, 176, 177
detrimental effects, 178, 179
direction, 175, 176
indecision, 180
learning/correction/iteration, 177
loop
acts, 181
adapt, 182
mental model, 181
sense/decide, 181
team-level decisiveness, 183
models, 183
operational trust, 171
overview, 189
Predictable Ops rules, 172–174
reverse logistics system, 179, 180
Deep learning, 212
tools, 16, 147, 191, 212

F, G, H

Field guide, 195–207
Financial tools, 79
Future proof
artificial intelligence (AI), 226, 227
business, 157, 158
executive briefing center, 154
industry analysts/influencers, 155
industry-specific roundtables, 154
internal reverse mentoring, 156
IT operations, 168
labs/free trials, 155
meaning, 151
organizational decisions, 168
overview, 189
podcasts, 155
preparation and foresight mode, 152, 169

INDEX

Future proof (*cont.*)
  roadmap
    business peers, 165
    Cloud-First approach, 167
    collaboration, 165
    experiment/operational
      reality, 166
    foundations/rules, 163, 164
    progress/
      transformation, 162
    time-constrained, 164
    vendors and service
      providers, 165
  roadmap briefings, 155
  strategic decisions, 154–157
  summaries, 155
  technical conferences, 154
  technology landscape, 160–162
  tracking industry trends/
    planning, 158
  transformation, 169
  transformative trends, 151
  trends/business values, 157–160

I, J

IT Service Management (ITSM), 49

K

Key Performance Indicators
  (KPIs), 25
  AI platform, 40
  correlation, 38
  customers, 32, 33
  dashboards, 28
  definition, 30
  deliberate process, 30
  indentification, 34, 35
  initial logs, 39
  mapping services, 31, 32
  predictable review, 38
  reviews, 37–40
  standardize and aggregate, 35
  tracking tools, 36, 37
  track performance, 28

L

Large Language Models (LLMs),
  44, 46, 212, *See also*
  Retrieval-Augmented
  Generation (RAG)

M, N

Machine learning (ML)
  data analysis, 211
  observability tools, 44
  tools, 16
MBRs, *see* Monthly Business
  Reviews (MBRs)
Measurement, 25
  artificial intelligence (AI),
    219–221
  ChatGPT homepage, 48–50
  dashboards
    intelligence, 43–46

INDEX

meaning, 40
observability, 41
predictive patterns, 41, 42
vanity dashboard, 42
decision support, 43-46
KPIs (*see* Key Performance
  Indicators (KPIs))
overview, 188
problem management
  definition, 49
  fixing recurring problems, 50
  root cause, 51
  solving problems, 49
  tools, 50
RAG/LLMs, 46, 47
Metrics/KPIs
  data correlation, 38
  definition, 29
  identification, 34
  KPI (*see* Key Performance
    Indicators (KPIs))
  observability, 41
ML, *see* Machine learning (ML)
Monthly Business Reviews (MBRs), 111, 112

O

Operations
  anomaly detection, 16
  artificial intelligence, 2
  clear expectations, 10
  documentation, 17
    categories, 17
    diagrams, 17
    hallucinations, 18
    legal/industry
      requirement, 19
    policies, 17
    runbooks, 17
    ticketing systems, 17
  downtime, 7-9
  efficiencies, 13, 14
  environment, 13
  foundational questions, 3
  insight tools, 14
  overview, 187
  performance
    degradation, 10, 11
  productivity, 12
  real-world app, 15
  recurring complaints, 8
  reliability, 1
  repeatable patterns, 3
  resiliency, 9, 10
  support availability, 4-7
  teams/partners, 2

P

Predictable Ops
  action, 193
  automation, 20
  blueprint, 23-25, 231
  collaboration, 21
  decisive leaders, 172-174
  deployment, 21
  humans, 193

245

INDEX

Predictable Ops (*cont.*)
    monitoring, 20
    operations (*see* Operations)
    preparation/insight, 190
    reflection, 193
    stability/trust/
        communication, 189
    ticketing tools, 20
    tooling categories, 20, 21

Q

Quarterly Business Reviews
    (QBRs), 104, 111, 112

R

Reliability, 1–3, 137
Retrieval-Augmented Generation
    (RAG), 46, 47, 212, 213
Return on investment (ROI), 96, 97
    benefits, 96
    factors, 96
    tool consolidation, 97
Reverse logistics system, 179, 180

S

Service Level Agreements
    (SLAs), 33, 34
Service Level Objectives
    (SLOs), 33, 34
Service process
    accountability tracker, 234–236

Audience Tiers Comms
    Matrix, 235
common ops tools, 232
complaints ledger, 228, 229
decisive loop, 237
roadmap table, 235, 236
team skills matrix, 232, 233
template, 230–233

T, U

Team development
    accountability
        accessibility, 62
        availability, 63
        definition, 57–59
        evolution, 61
        operational
            leadership, 60, 61
        past operations, 59
        regular check-ins, 61–63
        root access, 63
        task tracker/assignment, 58
    artificial intelligence (AI),
        221, 222
    balance edge and empathy, 77
    capabilities, 54
    change *vs.*
        empowerment, 75, 76
    definition, 55
    essential aspects, 68
    evaluation, 70
    front-line team, 70
    gaps

INDEX

capabilities, 71, 72
    prompt engineering, 71
    upskilling, 73, 74
gaps/blind spots, 56
non-real-time analysis, 69
operational trust, 53, 54
overview, 188
partners *vs.* vendors, 55
reward curiosity, 78
skills evolution table, 76
track capabilities, 68–71
trust/support team
    advice, 65
    bullets publicly, 64
    delegation, 63
    ideation and
        improvement, 67
    mistakes, 65, 66
work partners, 55, 56
Trusted partners, 127
    AI pitch, 144–146
    artificial intelligence (AI), 225, 226
    customer service, 147
    departments, 146
    facilities/real estate, 147
    finance/budgeting, 147
    human connection, 131, 132
    human resources, 147
    lead transformation, 146–148
    legal and compliance, 147
    marketing and sales, 147
    outcomes, 128
    overview, 188
    petabytes, 142
    priorities align
        aligning direction, 138
        alignment, 138, 139
        goals, 138
        real conversations, 141
        senior leader, 140
    quality assurance/testing, 146
    relationships, 134–136
    security operations, 146
    software engineering, 146
    transformation, 137, 138, 142, 143
    transparency matter, 133, 134
    trust-generating behaviors, 129, 130
    ultimate trust tests, 141
    unpredictable relationships, 133, 134

V, W, X, Y, Z

Value Added Resellers (VARs), 88, 91–93

GPSR Compliance

The European Union's (EU) General Product Safety Regulation (GPSR) is a set of rules that requires consumer products to be safe and our obligations to ensure this.

If you have any concerns about our products, you can contact us on

ProductSafety@springernature.com

In case Publisher is established outside the EU, the EU authorized representative is:

Springer Nature Customer Service Center GmbH
Europaplatz 3
69115 Heidelberg, Germany

www.ingramcontent.com/pod-product-compliance
Lightning Source LLC
LaVergne TN
LVHW021956060526
838201LV00048B/1593